Kathleen Perry

the everyday gourmet ®

Over 150 fast & easy gourmet recipes from TV's favorite cook!

To Harriett,
With best wishes
for happy cooking.
It's easy to be an
everyday gourmet!

Kathleen Perry

WARNER BOOKS
A Warner Communications Company

A Madison Press Book

Warner Books Inc.
666 Fifth Avenue
New York, N.Y. 10103

 A Warner Communications Company

First printing: June 1986

Design: David Shaw/Bookends East
Editorial: Hugh Brewster & Shelley Tanaka
Food testing: Alicia Homrich
Cover photography: Theodore Flagg
Illustrations: Elaine Macpherson

Library of Congress Cataloging-in-Publication Data

Perry, Kathleen.
  The everyday gourmet.

  "A Madison Press book."
  Includes index.
  1. Cookery.   I. Title.
TX715.P4697   1986   641.5   86-11108
ISBN 0-446-38095-4 (U.S.A.)(pbk.)
     0-446-38096-2 (Canada)(pbk.)

Produced by
Madison Press Books
40 Madison Avenue
Toronto, Ontario
Canada M5R 2S1

Printed and bound in Canada by D.W. Friesen Ltd.

For Bernard, my husband and best friend,
and for Betsy, our Super-kid,
who endured more than their share of "test kitchen,"
with my love and gratitude for their help, encouragement,
and especially for their good humor when
it wasn't easy to be living with an everyday gourmet!

Acknowledgments

Writing a cookbook is a series of tests. My talented daughter, Betsy, passed the test. For months she cooked for herself or ate out while *hearing* how easy it is to be an everyday gourmet.

If grades were given for excellence, my dear friend and associate, Alicia Homrich, would have earned an A-plus. She tested all the recipes with me while I, in turn, tested her patience to the limit with my weird jokes and Spoonerisms.

Now it's back to the *real* test—packing high school lunches, letting the cat in and out, ironing shirts and once again convincing my family that I am indeed an everyday gourmet.

the everyday gourmet.

About the Author

Kathleen Perry is the host of the TV program, *the everyday gourmet.*® In each fast-paced show, Kathleen's time-saving kitchen hints and easy-to-follow recipes show viewers how to add a touch of gourmet flair to their everyday cooking.

Trained as a home economist and teacher, Kathleen has a wide range of experience in the culinary field and has been the director of a cooking school and a consultant to a number of food-related companies. She has also studied at such prestigious cooking schools as Le Cordon Bleu and La Varenne in Paris.

As a wife and working mother, Kathleen discovered some years ago that what she and so many people she knew needed most of all were easy, tasty dishes that they could prepare simply and quickly for their families and friends. As "*the everyday gourmet*®" Kathleen now shows thousands of busy cooks just how fast and easy good cooking can be.

Kathleen is a certified member of the International Association of Cooking Professionals, and a member of the American Institute of Wine and Food, the American Home Economics Association and Home Economists in Business. She is married and lives with her husband and teenaged daughter in Orlando, Florida.

Contents

Introduction

"I *read* lots of cookbooks, but I actually *make* your recipes." Those flattering words have been echoed in lovely letters that I have received from my television show viewers and in many conversations with my cooking school students. It is my hope that you will both *read* this cookbook and *make* my recipes so that you, too, can discover how really easy it is to be an everyday gourmet.

I love to cook and I know how to cook. But when I've had a busy, tiring day and my family is hungry, the last thing I want to do is even think about tackling some complicated dish for dinner. The classic gourmet recipes that I love so much take much too long to make. Some time ago I realized that I could manage the time to prepare fancy gourmet dishes only once or twice a year. So I decided to find a simpler way to make these recipes so that we could enjoy them more often. That's how I became an everyday gourmet, and I'd like to share with you how easy it is for you to be one, too. You'll find that even adding a few new dishes to your usual selections is rewarding for you personally and lots more pleasing for your family. And that's really what it's all about, isn't it?

What's this book about?

This book is not meant to be Home Ec 101 or an exhaustive (and exhausting) compilation of every way to cook everything. It doesn't tell you how to organize your life or your kitchen. (When I get my own act together, *then* I'll tell you how to do that!) It won't send you on an expensive shopping spree to get the perfect pots and pans. You can make these recipes right now, no matter *what* you use to cook with. You'll find no call for exotic ingredients that your local supermarket doesn't carry; in fact, you probably have most of the ingredients in the house already.

In developing these recipes, I've tried to simplify procedures and uncomplicate each dish. When a store-bought ingredient is as good as or more convenient than making it from scratch, I've suggested that you use a mix or prepared product. I've made every one of the recipes in this book many times and have been pleased to serve them to my family and friends. They are not designed to be budget recipes, nor are they excessive or extravagant. No matter who you are—woman or man, single or married, young or old—there are times when you will need to be cooking. Whether you are an experienced cook or brand new at it, I'm sure you will find these dishes appealing, worthwhile and surprisingly simple to prepare.

Far too many people tell me they know how to cook five things for dinner and that they have them every week. (I guess they eat out, send out, or have leftovers for the other two days.) That's okay, but the "if this is meatloaf it must be Tuesday" routine gets to be very boring, both for you and everyone you're feeding. Now I'm not knocking meatloaf—far from it—but it's much more fun and lots more satisfying to try some different things, too.

How long do these recipes take? Well, if the phone doesn't ring, the dog doesn't have to go out, the paper carrier doesn't want to be paid, the clothes dryer doesn't die and nobody ate the ingredients you need, then everyday gourmet meals with special touches won't take any longer to make than meatloaf.

Basic Assets

One thing that really annoys me about some cookbooks is that when you're all set to make a recipe, you discover that it calls for "½ cup of something on page 10." That something takes three days and a butcher shop full of bones to make. There are no recipes like that in this book.

However, one of the most important parts of this book is the first section called "everyday basics." There you'll find six delicious combinations of ingredients that—once you've made them and have them on hand—will save you more time and effort than you can imagine. These basics are used in many of the recipes in this book, and nothing could be easier or quicker to make. In fact, making out the shopping list for the everyday basics is the hardest part—and I've already done that for you (p.26)! I've even included easy food processor instructions so you don't have to wash out the bowl between recipes! (What are friends for?) So, raise your right hand and repeat after me: "I promise to make the six everyday basic recipes as soon as possible." And *I* promise that you'll be very glad you did!

Machine Cuisine

I said that you could make any recipe in this book right now with whatever kitchen equipment you have, and that is true. There is just one thing that I would like to suggest to make your life in the kitchen much easier—a food processor! It's like having an extra pair of hands in the kitchen. As with most things you buy, the quality depends pretty much on what you pay for, so buy the best you can afford, or put a new processor on the top of your gift list. If you don't have a food processor, a mixer, blender or just a whisk will do the job—for now.

Freeze Now, Feast Later

No matter how much we might enjoy cooking, there are days when what we'd like to make for dinner is a restaurant reservation. The next best thing is to have dinner "reserved" in the freezer. It takes very little extra effort to double or triple a recipe. Since you have the ingredients out anyway, just make the extra batches while you're at it. Your own "convenience foods" will especially come in handy when there's too much month left at the end of the money. Just don't forget to thaw!

Almost anything can be frozen if it's done right. I've included lots of freezing tips plus other useful Everyday Hints that are marked with a whisk throughout this book. With most recipes, I've also suggested some other ideas and variations for you to consider.

Breaking Bread

Opening your home and your heart to family and friends is a beautiful way to let them know you care about them. In the last chapter of the book, "When Company Comes," you'll find suggestions and ideas to help make family celebrations and get-togethers with friends extra special.

Even though we have more time-saving conveniences than our parents and grandparents had, we often find that life today is very complicated and that we don't have enough time to do the things that are really important. Family life and friendships can become fragmented because it's difficult to keep up with everyone's activities and to touch base with their needs and feelings. That's why meal time is so important—frequently it's the only time we can be with one another.

Adventure in the kitchen is much more fun than mealtime monotony, so don't be afraid to try new things. In this book, I've given you a few basics, some good ideas and lots of wonderful, easy recipes to get you started. All you have to do is make one or two of them, and, as you listen to the compliments from everyone at your table, just smile and say, "It's *easy* to be an everyday gourmet!"

—Kathleen Perry

Everyday Basics

Not one of these everyday basics is difficult to make. In fact, I can't think of anything that takes so little effort yet brings such great rewards. They're just wonderful time-savers when everyone is starving and you're the chief cook.

Most people have favorite flavors and foods that they tend to choose whether they are cooking at home or eating out. If you prefer to substitute other flavoring ingredients in your everyday basic recipes, by all means delete or add whatever you like. That's the beauty of having basic recipes on hand—you know they've been made exactly to your taste, and there's no guesswork involved.

For those days when you think your brain has gone on vacation or you're too tired to think, having these basics at your fingertips allows you to work like a robot. (You will know it's one of those days when you've made three trips to the garage and you still can't remember what you went there for!)

Store or freeze your everyday basics in the portions that you would normally use for a recipe. I buy inexpensive disposable plastic cups or containers with lids (like the ones used for take-out salads at the deli or meat counter). They are available in all sizes, so you can pre-measure the quantity you want before freezing, and then thaw only what you need. You can find disposable containers at party supply stores, but first check your Yellow Pages for wholesale paper supply companies. They usually have an outlet where you can buy smaller amounts at greatly reduced prices.

Many liquid and dry ingredients freeze best in snap-type plastic freezer bags. They stack flat and take up less freezer space than other containers. Write directly on the bag or container with a permanent ink felt-tip marker. This way you won't end up with a collection of "mystery" packages because the labels have fallen off in the freezer. Unless your memory is much better than mine, throw in a note with the dry mixes to remind yourself what other ingredients to add and at what temperature to bake them. This will save you from having to check the recipe.

Many kitchen jobs take only a minute or two each, but added together can become a big chore. That's why I try to do little things like sift the confectioner's sugar directly into an airtight container so it's ready to go, and store the brown sugar the same way so I don't have to fight the box, reclose the plastic bag and clean up the spilled sugar each time I use it. In addition to the six basics, another thing that I find to be a big help when every minute counts is to pre-mix frequently used ingredient combinations— things like cinnamon-sugar and Streusel Topping (p. 117), dry ingredients for muffins and pie dough, Homemade Tomato Sauce (p. 101) and Herb Mayonnaise (p. 87).

Herb Butter

If you make only one thing from this book, Herb Butter has got to be it. It's so easy to do that you'll never want to be without it. Herb Butter is a delicious complement to any meal. You can spread it on bread, but it's equally at home on a baked potato or vegetable, great on steak, fish, poultry or pasta, and will perk up any sauce or gravy.

1   **cup butter (2 sticks), softened**
1   **tablespoon lemon juice**
1   **tablespoon minced parsley**
1   **clove garlic, finely minced**

With a food processor: With the machine running, drop the parsley and garlic into the feed tube to mince them. Stop the machine, add the butter and lemon juice and process the mixture until well blended.

With an electric mixer: In a bowl, beat the butter until it is fluffy, then beat in the lemon juice, minced parsley and minced garlic until all the ingredients are well blended.

Along one side of a 12-inch piece of wax paper or plastic wrap, evenly spread half of the Herb Butter to about the same size and shape as a stick of butter, then roll it up evenly. Repeat with the remaining Herb Butter, then refrigerate it for 1 hour to allow the flavors to develop and blend.

I like to make several recipes of Herb Butter from the basic recipe, divide it into smaller portions, then add different herbs to each portion and label them accordingly.

Make a variety of Herb Butters to enhance specific foods. Just add 1 tablespoon fresh or 1 teaspoon dried herbs to the basic recipe. Cut the garlic in half or omit it, if you prefer.

Make: dill butter for seafood
        tarragon butter for poultry
        basil butter for pasta
        mint butter for lamb
        rosemary butter for pork
        chive butter for vegetables

Herb Butter will be the most important and most versatile staple in your refrigerator and it freezes beautifully. I like to freeze it in the shape of a regular stick of butter so it's easier to measure. Just wrap it in plastic wrap or aluminum foil.

Herb Butter is used in these recipes:

Cheesy Herb Bread (p. 33)
Chicken Rollups (p. 51)
Chicken Pot Pie (p. 52)
Chicken à la King (p. 53)
Chicken Divan (p. 54)
Shrimp in Scampi Sauce (p. 55)
Cornish Hens (p. 57)
Savory Apricot Sauce (p. 57)
Medallions of Turkey with Mushroom Tarragon Sauce (p. 58)
Pan Gravy (p. 60)
Pork with Apple Onion Sauce (p. 61)
Beef Burgundy (p. 62)
Beef Stroganoff (p. 63)
Everyday Béarnaise Sauce (p. 66)
Homemade Seasoned Croutons (p. 93)
Potato Wedgies (p. 104)
Potatoes Parmesan (p. 104)
Herb White Sauce (p. 107)
Cheddar Cheese Sauce (p. 107)
Herb Biscuits (p. 111)

 Everyday Hint: Before adding dried herbs to a recipe, rub them between the palms of your hands or crush them with your fingertips to release the herb flavor. 1 teaspoon dried herbs equals 1 tablespoon fresh herbs.

 Everyday Hint: Squeeze the juice from fresh lemon halves through your fingers. This way the seeds go in your hand and not into the other ingredients.

Seasoned Bread Crumbs

Seasoned Bread Crumbs provide a savory coating for meats and fish and a flavorful, crunchy topping for casseroles and vegetables. I especially like to use French, Italian or homemade-style breads.

2	**cups bread crumbs (about 4 bread slices)**
2	**tablespoons minced parsley**
1	**clove garlic, finely minced**
1	**teaspoon salt**
1/2	**teaspoon pepper**
1	**teaspoon dried herbs such as basil, oregano, thyme etc. (or 1 tablespoon chopped fresh)**

To make the crumbs, tear the bread slices into small pieces and place them in a blender or food processor. Make bread crumbs by turning the machine on and off until the crumbs are small and uniform in size. Add the parsley, garlic, salt, pepper and herbs to the crumbs and process again to mix them thoroughly. Store the Seasoned Bread Crumbs in a plastic freezer bag in the freezer. Makes 2 cups.

Parmesan Bread Crumbs

These have all the goodness of Seasoned Bread Crumbs but with the wonderful flavor of Parmesan cheese. (You don't have to be Italian to love them!)

1	**recipe** *Seasoned Bread Crumbs (see above)*
1	**cup grated Parmesan cheese**

Mix Seasoned Bread Crumbs and Parmesan cheese together. Store the Parmesan Bread Crumbs in plastic freezer bags in the freezer.

The fresh flavor of homemade Seasoned Bread Crumbs far surpasses the strong, over-seasoned flavor of most of the crumbs you buy. And when you figure that 1 slice of bread makes about 1/2 cup of crumbs, the bought kind are outrageously expensive. Make your own from leftover rolls, biscuits or any unsweetened bread. Store the bread in the freezer until you have enough for a batch of crumbs.

For homemade bread crumbs, it's best to use bread that is two to four days old. If the bread is fresh the crumbs may clump together, so heat the crumbs in a baking pan in a 300 degree oven to dry them out before adding seasonings. If you prefer toasted crumbs, bake them an extra few minutes until they're lightly browned. Toasted crumbs are especially desirable for microwaving since they add crispness and color. After the crumbs have cooled add any herbs or Parmesan or Romano cheese to the crumbs if desired.

Seasoned Bread Crumbs or Parmesan Bread Crumbs are used in these recipes:

Chicken Parmesan Drumettes (p. 42) and Nuggets (p. 43)
Chicken Rollups (p. 51)
Chicken Parmesan (p. 55)
Shrimp in Scampi Sauce (p. 55)
Fillet of Flounder Pinwheels (p. 67)
Oven-baked Pasta (p. 74)
Hot Potato Salad (p. 92)
Tomatoes Florentine (p. 100)
Tomato Mousse (p. 101)
Potatoes Parmesan (p. 104)

 Everyday Hint: Use scissors to chop parsley or other fresh herbs. Place the herbs in a glass measuring cup and snip away! There's no mess because the herbs stay in the cup, and it's easier to measure them.

Garlic Oil

Garlic Oil has a mellower flavor and a better taste than raw garlic. Use it any time a recipe calls for fresh garlic. Besides tasting great, the garlic flavors the oil and not your fingers.

1	**bulb garlic (8 to 12 cloves)**
2	**cups oil**

To peel the garlic, lay the flat side of a kitchen knife on top of a garlic clove. With your fist, lightly pound the top of the knife to slightly flatten the garlic and loosen the skin. Remove the skin and place the garlic cloves in a jar with a lid.

Pour in the oil and refrigerate for a day or two to allow the flavor to develop. If you prefer a more pronounced flavor, crush a garlic clove before adding it to the oil. Makes 2 cups.

You can substitute Garlic Oil any time a recipe calls for fresh garlic:

1 tablespoon Garlic Oil = 1 clove garlic

When Garlic Oil is stored in the refrigerator, it will keep for weeks. Just replenish the oil as you use it. If the flavor becomes too strong, remove the garlic cloves from the oil. If it begins to lose its flavor, just make a fresh batch of Garlic Oil.

Use Garlic Oil for sautéing:
Meats, fish or vegetables have a subtle garlic flavor without the bitterness of burned garlic pieces.

Use Garlic Oil for salad dressings:
Garlic Oil is a great addition to salad dressings. Just replace part of the oil in Vinaigrette (p. 83) or other dressings with Garlic Oil and leave out the minced garlic.

Use Garlic Oil for flavoring:
Mix Garlic Oil with butter or other ingredients for a marvelous spread for breads or crackers, or use it in place of the garlic in Herb Butter (p. 18). Use part Garlic Oil in marinades or for basting meats while cooking.

 Everyday Hint: When buying garlic, choose firm bulbs with unbroken skins. Avoid soft, shriveled or sprouting garlic bulbs, which will have a bitter flavor.

Alfredo Sauce

This magnificent sauce is a heavenly blend of butter, heavy cream and Parmesan cheese that traditionally is combined at the last minute. But by making Alfredo Sauce the everyday gourmet way, it's ready to add to many pasta dishes—and some pasta-less dishes, too.

1	cup butter (2 sticks), softened
1	cup grated Parmesan cheese
1	cup heavy cream

Using a food processor or mixer, beat the butter until it is very light and fluffy. Beat in the Parmesan cheese, then gradually beat the cream into the mixture until it is completely absorbed. Makes 2½ cups sauce.

Store Alfredo Sauce in the refrigerator or freezer in recipe-sized portions. Most recipes in this book call for ½ cup Alfredo Sauce, so freeze it in ½-cup portions for easy use. Let the sauce come to room temperature before combining it with pasta or other foods.

Alfredo Sauce can be flavored with other herbs. Add basil and garlic to make a creamy and mellow Pesto Sauce (p. 73).

Alfredo Sauce is used in these recipes:

Fettuccine Alfredo (p. 72)
Fettuccine Alfredo Primavera (p. 72)
Straw and Hay Pasta (p. 73)
Fettuccine with Pesto Cream Sauce (p. 73)
Oven-baked Pasta (p. 74)
Linguine with Shrimp and Mushrooms (p. 75)
Vegetables in Alfredo Sauce (p. 105)

Herb Cheese

Redolent with garlic, this lively Herb Cheese is a great spread. But baked with meat or vegetables, it adds a new flavor dimension to the recipe. It's super on a sandwich—ham, roast beef, corned beef or even bologna.

1	**8-oz. package cream cheese, softened**
2	**tablespoons butter, softened**
1	**tablespoon finely minced parsley**
1	**small clove garlic, finely minced**
1	**tablespoon lemon juice**
¹/₄	**teaspoon salt**
	pepper

With a food processor: With the machine running, drop the parsley and garlic into the feed tube to mince them. Stop the machine, add the remaining ingredients and process the mixture until it is well blended.

With an electric mixer: Combine all the ingredients and beat well until the mixture is thoroughly combined.

Chill for 1 hour or more before serving so the flavors will develop and blend. Makes about 1 cup.

Add other fresh or dried herbs if you prefer—chives, dill, thyme, basil, rosemary, tarragon or coarsely ground pepper. Buy cream cheese when it's on sale and make lots of Herb Cheese to freeze in smaller portions.

Herb Cheese is used in these recipes:

Basic Biscuit Mix

Prepackaged baking mixes are terrific time-savers (and often life-savers) when you have to bake something in a hurry. But if you make your own biscuit mix—and it takes only minutes—you can control exactly what goes into it.

2	**cups flour**
1	**tablespoon baking powder**
¹/₂	**teaspoon salt**
¹/₂	**cup butter (1 stick), cold**

In a large bowl, thoroughly mix the flour, baking powder and salt. Using a food processor, pastry blender or two knives, cut in the butter until it is the size of very small peas and distributed throughout the dry ingredients.

For added convenience, make and package Basic Biscuit Mix in recipe-sized portions. If you are cooking for just one or two people, you might prefer to divide the Basic Biscuit Mix in half before freezing. Just remember to label the bag, so the other ingredients will be reduced by half when preparing the recipe. I like to use plastic snap-type freezer bags, so they can lie flat and stack in the freezer.

Traditionally, biscuits are made using lard or solid vegetable shortening. This recipe uses butter because I think the flavor is so much better, but do feel free to substitute vegetable shortening if you prefer to use it.

With just the addition of a liquid, Basic Biscuit Mix can be transformed into tender, flaky biscuits, tempting tea rings and sweet rolls, rich shortcakes or even pizza crusts. Homemade or Drop Biscuits make a delicious, tender topping for any casserole or fruit cobbler.

Basic Biscuit Mix is used in these recipes:

Quick Pizza (p. 45)
Chicken and Dumplings (p. 54)
Homemade Biscuits (p. 110)
Homemade Drop Biscuits (p. 111)
Buttermilk Biscuits (p. 111)
Cheese Biscuits (p. 111)
Herb Biscuits (p. 111)
Biscuit Tea Ring (p. 112)
Savory Biscuit Pinwheels (p. 113)
Biscuit Sweet Rolls (p. 114)
Shortcake (p. 139)
Fruit Cobbler (p. 140)

A Shopping List for the Everyday Basics

This ten-item shopping list contains everything you will need for making the six everyday basics. You probably have most of these ingredients on hand already. The amounts listed are enough to make three batches of Basic Biscuit Mix, two batches of Bread Crumbs (one Seasoned and one with Parmesan) and single recipes of Herb Butter, Garlic Oil, Alfredo Sauce and Herb Cheese.

_____	flour	2 pounds all-purpose
_____	vegetable oil	16 ounces
_____	bread	1 loaf (8 slices needed)
_____	Parmesan cheese	8 ounces
_____	cream cheese	8 ounces
_____	heavy cream	8 ounces (1 cup)
_____	butter	2 pounds
_____	garlic	2 bulbs (heads)
_____	lemons	2
_____	parsley	1 bunch

Pantry check list:

_____ baking powder

_____ your choice of dried herbs
(Suggestions: basil, oregano, dill, thyme or tarragon)

_____ salt

_____ pepper

Everyday Basics in a Food Processor

If you have a food processor, make the everyday basics in this order and you won't even have to wash the processor bowl between recipes. It should take less than an hour for you to make all six recipes.

Before starting have the cream cheese and 5 sticks of the butter at room temperature. Keep the remaining 3 sticks of butter cold.

1. **Basic Biscuit Mix**

   Make three recipes, one at a time.
   Place in three freezer bags, label and freeze.
   Wipe out the processor bowl with paper towels.

2. **Seasoned Bread Crumbs**

   Wash and dry parsley.
   Chop in the food processor.
   Remove from the processor bowl and set aside.
   Make two recipes.
   Place in two freezer bags.
   To one bag, mix in 1 cup Parmesan cheese.
   Label each bag and freeze.
   Wipe out the processor bowl with paper towels.

3. **Alfredo Sauce**

   Make one recipe.
   With a rubber spatula, scrape out the processor bowl.
   Divide into ½-cup portions, label and freeze.
   Wipe out the processor bowl with paper towels.

4. **Herb Butter**

   Make one recipe.
   With a rubber spatula, scrape out the processor bowl.
   Shape and refrigerate or freeze.

5. **Herb Cheese**

   Make one recipe.
   Remove from the bowl and refrigerate or freeze.

6. **Garlic Oil** (No food processor necessary)

   Peel all remaining garlic cloves.
   Drop them into the bottle of oil and refrigerate.

   Hooray... you're on your way to being an everyday gourmet!

Starters
and Snacks

This chapter covers everything from Vichyssoise (p. 38) to Toasted Pecans (p. 46). The only problem with these starters is that you won't want to stop eating them!

Guaranteed to please, this assortment of tasty tempters has something for everyone. Crunchy crudités and irresistible dips (p. 34) will keep you healthy and guilt-free about calories. Quick and zesty snacks and sandwiches hit the spot for TV snacking. Savory spreads are ideal for party fare. Satisfying soups like Cream of Watercress (p. 39) make an elegant first course for special dinners. And for those who crave sweet stuff, herein lies the best Caramel Popcorn (p. 47) you've ever tasted!

Herb Cheese Spread

Herb Cheese is a tasty spread for crackers and raw vegetables. I love it best heaped on crusty French bread and served with fresh fruit for a picnic lunch or light supper. It's as good as the high-priced imported cheese, but you can make it in minutes at a fraction of the cost. If you're practicing "girth" control, here's a lower-calorie version, too.

1   **recipe** *Herb Cheese (p. 24)*

Idea: To make "Girth Control" Herb Cheese, substitute Neufchatel (or low-calorie cream cheese) for the cream cheese and low-calorie sour dressing for the butter.

Idea: For variety, add other fresh or dried herbs to Herb Cheese, such as thyme, dill, chives, tarragon, rosemary, basil, etc.

Idea: To mold the Herb Cheese Spread, line a 1-cup straight-sided dish with plastic wrap. Pack the cheese into the dish, cover with plastic wrap and refrigerate for 1 hour or more to allow the cheese to firm and the flavors to develop and blend. Before serving, unmold the cheese, remove the plastic wrap and place on a serving dish.

Savory Cheddar Cheese Spread

The easiest way to make this robust-flavored cheese spread is in a food processor. It's especially enjoyable when served with fresh apple rings.

1	**pound cheddar cheese**
½	**cup butter (1 stick), softened**
1	**clove garlic, minced**
1	**teaspoon lemon juice**
1	**teaspoon Dijon mustard**
¼	**teaspoon Worcestershire sauce**
¼	**teaspoon pepper**
¼	**cup beer**
	chopped pecans, optional

With a food processor: Finely shred or chop the cheddar cheese. Add the butter, garlic, lemon juice, mustard, Worcestershire sauce, pepper and beer. Process until the mixture is well blended and smooth.

With an electric mixer: Finely shred the cheese and place it in the mixing bowl. Beat the cheese for 2 minutes to soften it. Beat in the butter, then the garlic, lemon juice, mustard, Worcestershire sauce, pepper and beer until the cheese mixture is smooth.

Mound the cheese spread into a crock or serving bowl, sprinkle with chopped pecans and refrigerate for 1 hour or more to allow the flavors to blend. Let the cheese soften to spreading consistency at room temperature before serving. Makes 2½ cups.

Swiss Pecan Wheel

Serve this mellow cheese spread with bland crackers so the delicate cheese flavor can be the star.

8	**ounces Swiss or Gruyère cheese**
1	**8-oz. package cream cheese, softened**
¹/₂	**clove garlic, minced**
1 to 2	**tablespoons Kirsch liqueur, optional**
1	**cup *Toasted Pecans (p. 46)***

With a food processor: Finely shred or chop the Swiss cheese. Add the cream cheese, garlic and Kirsch and process until the mixture is well blended and smooth. Add ¹/₂ cup Toasted Pecans and turn the processor on and off to chop the nuts.

With an electric mixer: Finely shred the Swiss cheese, place it in the mixing bowl and beat for 2 minutes to soften it. Beat in the cream cheese, then beat in the garlic and Kirsch until the mixture is smooth. Chop ¹/₂ cup Toasted Pecans and stir them into the cheese.

To make a cheese "wheel," line a straight-sided bowl with plastic wrap. Pack the cheese into the bowl, cover and refrigerate for 1 hour or more to allow the flavors to blend. Before serving, remove the plastic wrap, chop the remaining ¹/₂ cup Toasted Pecans and roll the cheese wheel in the pecans. Let the cheese soften to spreading consistency at room temperature before serving. Makes about 2 cups.

Idea: Instead of a wheel, shape the cheese spread into a mound and coat with chopped Toasted Pecans.

 Everyday Hint: Instead of crackers, spread any cheese on fresh apple rings for a different and tasty treat. Core unpeeled apples, slice them into ¹/₄-inch rings and dip them in lemon juice to keep them from discoloring. Arrange alternating slices of red and green apples on a serving plate with the cheese.

Mushroom Almond Pâté

The coarseness of this meatless spread gives it the look and texture of a country pâté. It tastes great spread on crusty bread or crispy crackers. With a food processor, you can make it in a jiffy.

2	tablespoons green onion (or onion)
1	pound fresh mushrooms
2	tablespoons butter
2	tablespoons lemon juice
1/2	teaspoon dried tarragon
1/2	teaspoon salt
1/4	teaspoon pepper
2	cups almonds (10 ounces), toasted
1	tablespoon dry sherry wine
1/4	cup butter (1/2 stick), softened
1/4	cup heavy cream

In a food processor, chop the green onion and remove from the processor bowl. Put the mushrooms in the food processor bowl, process until finely chopped and set aside.

In a large skillet over medium heat, melt the 2 tablespoons butter and cook the green onion until soft. Add the chopped mushrooms, lemon juice, tarragon, salt and pepper. Raise the heat to high and cook the mixture, stirring frequently, until almost all of the liquid has evaporated. The mixture should be slightly moist. Set aside.

In the food processor, chop the almonds until finely ground. Add the mushroom mixture, sherry, 1/4 cup butter and cream. Continue processing for about 2 minutes until the mixture is very smooth.

Pack the pâté into a serving bowl or crock, or shape it into a mound. Cover it with plastic wrap and chill thoroughly. To serve, place the pâté on a serving dish and garnish it with additional almonds if desired. Spread on crackers or crusty bread. Makes 2 1/2 cups.

Red Radish Spread

If you don't tell, nobody will ever guess that radishes are the main ingredient in this marvelous, tangy spread. I love it on French bread, but it's super on crackers, too.

1	8-oz. package cream cheese, softened
¹/₂	cup butter (1 stick), softened
¹/₂	teaspoon celery seed
¹/₂	teaspoon Worcestershire sauce
1	cup red radishes
¹/₄	cup green onion (white part only)

With a food processor: Chop the radishes and green onion and remove from the processor bowl. Place the cream cheese, butter, celery seed and Worcestershire sauce in the processor bowl and blend thoroughly. Add the radishes and green onion to the cheese mixture and process just until combined. Chill.

With an electric mixer: Beat together the cream cheese, butter, celery seed and Worcestershire sauce. Very finely mince the radishes and the green onion, and blend them into the cheese mixture. Chill. Makes 2 cups.

 Everyday Hint: Serve your favorite dips or spreads in hollowed-out vegetables—red or green peppers, squashes, cabbages, eggplant, etc., and refill them as needed. For a decorative touch, carve the vegetable opening into scallops or points. Choose vegetable colors that complement the color of the dip.

Cheesy Herb Bread

This flavorful bread takes seconds to fix and works wonders in livening up an everyday meal. It's especially satisfying when served with a salad for lunch or a light supper.

1	loaf French bread
	Herb Butter (p. 18)
	cheddar cheese, grated or very thinly sliced

Preheat oven to 350 degrees.

Cut a loaf of French bread in half lengthwise. Spread the cut surface of each half with a generous amount of softened Herb Butter. Sprinkle a small amount of grated or thinly sliced cheese over the butter. Heat the bread on a baking sheet for 10 minutes or until the bread is crisp and the cheese melts.

Crudités

I love to say "crudités." The French word (pronounced kru-dee-táy) *sounds so much more elegant than "raw vegetables," and crudités are a healthy alternative to the chip and pretzel habit. Use any vegetable and vary the colors and shapes—like Radish Jacks, Switcheroos and Radish Mums—for a more attractive platter.*

Blanching some vegetables briefly in boiling water brings out their color and flavor and makes them easier to digest. Refreshing them quickly in cold water stops the cooking and leaves them crunchy and tender-crisp.

Suggested vegetables:

Blanched	*Raw*
asparagus	celery
broccoli	cherry tomatoes
carrots	mushrooms
cauliflower	radishes
green beans	red or green peppers
	zucchini or yellow squash

Blanch vegetables by dropping bite-sized pieces into boiling water for 1 to 3 minutes, depending on the thickness of the vegetable. Drain the vegetables and refresh them by immediately plunging them into ice-cold water for several minutes to stop the cooking and to crisp them. Drain them well.

To blanch 1 pound of vegetables in the microwave, place bite-sized pieces in a microwave-safe casserole with ¼ cup water and cover with a lid or microwave plastic wrap that has been folded back to vent it at one edge. Microwave on high power for 3 to 5 minutes. Immediately plunge the vegetables into cold water for several minutes and drain well.

Radish Jacks
Slice radish circles about ⅛ inch thick. Make a slit from the outside edge to the center of each radish circle. Intersect the two circles together at the slits. Radish Jacks make good scoopers for dips.

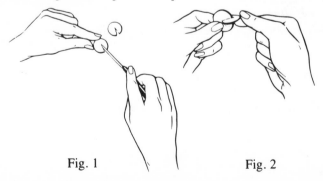

Fig. 1   Fig. 2

Switcheroos

With a tiny cookie cutter, cut out the centers of two different vegetable slices. Switch the centers to "invent" a new vegetable. Use radishes, carrots, squash or cucumber slices.

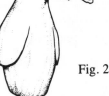

Squash Birds

They're fun to make and add a whimsical touch to vegetable platters or any food tray. Choose large and small crookneck squash with some "personality" and nicely shaped "beaks" (stems). (Don't worry if they look at you kind of funny at the produce counter!) Cut off about ½ inch from the bottom so the squash can stand.

To make the wings, cut a thin slice up each side of the squash, leaving the top of the slice attached. With the knife tip, carefully wedge a thin sliver of leftover squash under each wing to hold wings out from the body.

For the eyes, insert a whole clove or peppercorn on each side of the beak.

Make Squash Birds of different heights and arrange them around a Vegetable Tree (p. 150) or on a vegetable platter.

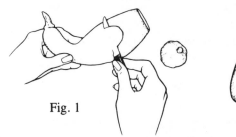

Fig. 1   Fig. 2

Radish Mums

To make a Radish Mum, cut off the root and stem end of a large red radish. With a sharp, thin knife, make about 12 cuts very close together and halfway through the root end of the radish. Rotate the radish and make the same number of cuts, very close together, in the opposite direction. Place the cut Radish Mum in ice water for at least 1 hour for the "flower" to open.

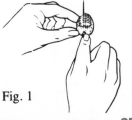

Fig. 1   Fig. 2

Herb Mayonnaise Dip

This combination has just the right consistency for dipping and the right blend of flavors for serving with crudités, shrimp, chips or other snacks.

1	cup *Herb Mayonnaise (p. 87)*
1	cup sour cream

Thoroughly blend the Herb Mayonnaise and sour cream together in a bowl. Refrigerate the mixture to allow the flavors to blend. Makes 2 cups.

Idea: Make Curry Dip by adding ¼ to ½ teaspoon curry powder to the Herb Mayonnaise Dip.

Hot Spinach Cheese Dip

This flavorful dip is best when served hot. It provides a pleasant and unexpected contrast in temperature when accompanying raw vegetables.

1	10-oz. package frozen chopped spinach, thawed
1	cup softened *Herb Cheese (p. 24)*
1	cup shredded Swiss cheese (4 ounces)
1	cup sour cream
1	tablespoon chopped onion
1	teaspoon Dijon mustard
½	teaspoon salt
¼	teaspoon pepper

Preheat oven to 350 degrees.

Squeeze the water out of the spinach. In an ovenproof bowl, stir together the spinach, Herb Cheese, Swiss cheese, sour cream, onion, mustard, salt and pepper. Bake the mixture for 15 to 20 minutes or just until the Swiss cheese has melted. Serve the dip hot, warm or at room temperature.

To microwave: Place all the ingredients in a microwave-safe bowl. Microwave on high power for 2 minutes. Stir, microwave 2 more minutes and stir again. Microwave another minute or just until the Swiss cheese has melted and the mixture is hot. Makes about 3 cups.

Cheese Puffs

These light and airy morsels of goodness are just tiny cheese-flavored cream puffs. Make them for a tempting and tasty cocktail accompaniment.

¹/₄	**cup butter (¹/₂ stick)**
¹/₂	**cup water**
¹/₂	**cup flour**
2	**eggs**
³/₄	**cup grated Swiss or Gruyère cheese (3 ounces)**
1	**teaspoon Dijon or whole-grain mustard**
¹/₄	**teaspoon salt**
¹/₄	**teaspoon pepper**
	few drops of hot pepper sauce

Preheat oven to 400 degrees.

In a small saucepan over high heat, bring the butter and water to a rolling boil. Add the flour all at once and stir vigorously until the mixture forms a ball. Continue to cook for 1 minute, stirring constantly, until the dough dries slightly and leaves a light film on the bottom of the pan.

Remove the pan from the heat. Using a hand mixer or spoon beat in 1 egg, until it is absorbed. Add the second egg and continue beating until the dough is smooth and shiny. Stir in the cheese, mustard, salt, pepper and hot pepper sauce.

On an ungreased baking sheet, drop teaspoonfuls of the cheese mixture, placing them 2 inches apart. Bake for 20 to 25 minutes until puffed and well browned. Do not underbake or the puffs will collapse. Makes about 36 puffs.

Vichyssoise

Nothing beats the earthy flavors of leeks and potatoes brought to perfection in a wonderfully cool and creamy Vichyssoise topped with a sprinkling of chopped chives. This easy, versatile soup is a basis for any vegetable cream soup and tastes even better the second day.

3	tablespoons butter
2	cups leeks (2 to 3 medium), white part only, cleaned and sliced
2	cups potatoes (4 medium), peeled and chopped
5	cups chicken broth
1	cup heavy cream
	salt and pepper to taste

In a large saucepan with a lid, heat the butter over low heat. Stir in the leeks and cover the pan. Cook for 5 to 10 minutes until the leeks are soft but not brown, stirring occasionally.

Stir the potatoes and chicken broth into the leeks, raise the heat and bring the mixture to a boil. Lower the heat, cover the pan and simmer the soup until the potatoes are very soft, about 30 minutes. Take the pan off the heat, remove the lid and let the soup cool.

In small batches, puree the soup in a blender, food processor or food mill. Transfer the soup to a large bowl as it is pureed. (The soup can be made to this point 1 to 2 days ahead and refrigerated.)

Stir the soup to mix it well, then stir in the cream. If you prefer, half-and-half or milk can be substituted for the cream, but the soup will not have the same rich flavor. Add salt and pepper to taste. Refrigerate and serve chilled. Makes about 2 quarts.

Everyday Hint: Leeks are often full of sand and dirt and must be washed thoroughly before using them in any recipe. To clean leeks, cut off the root end and the green stems. Cut the leek in half lengthwise and rinse it under cold, running water until all traces of dirt are removed. Shake the leeks dry.

Cream of Watercress Soup

The peppery flavor of watercress gives a pleasant and distinctive bite to this cold soup. The delicate green color makes it equally appealing to the eye.

1	recipe *Vichyssoise (p. 38)*
1	bunch watercress (about 2 cups lightly packed)

Wash the watercress and remove the coarse stems.

Prepare the recipe for Vichyssoise, except add the watercress in the last few minutes of simmering and before pureeing the soup. Stir in the cream and chill before serving. Garnish the soup with fresh watercress leaves. Makes about 2 quarts.

Idea: For "Cream of *Any* Vegetable Soup" add a cup or more of cooked vegetables to the Vichyssoise recipe before pureeing. It's a great way to use leftover vegetables.

Everyday Hint: Before pureeing creamed soups, reserve a small amount of the cooked vegetable to use as an attractive garnish. In the center of each serving, spoon a dollop of unsweetened whipped cream or sour cream and sprinkle with a pinch of coarse salt. On top of the cream, place a small floret of broccoli or cauliflower, criss-crossed carrot sticks, an asparagus tip, a sprig of fresh herbs, or any other touch that is compatible with the ingredients in the soup.

Everyday Hint: Cold cream soups are just as delicious served hot. Warm the soup slowly just to simmer it. The soup should not come to a boil after the cream has been added.

Stuffed Mushroom Caps

Baked mushrooms are special by themselves, but topped with these delicious fillings they are out of this world!

1   **pound fresh mushrooms (medium to large size)**
1   **recipe filling (see below)**

Preheat oven to 400 degrees.

Clean the mushrooms and cut the stems off straight across at the base of the mushroom. This provides the cooked mushrooms with support so they won't flatten out during cooking and won't collapse when picked up.

In a shallow baking pan, place the mushroom caps with the stem side up. Spoon filling on top of each mushroom cap and shape it into a mound.

Bake for 10 to 12 minutes or until the mushrooms and filling are just heated through. Do not overcook them. Serve the mushrooms hot. Makes 6 to 8 appetizers or side dishes.

To microwave: Arrange half of the stuffed caps in a hollow circle on a paper towel-lined baking dish. Microwave them for 2 minutes on high power. Let the mushrooms stand for 5 minutes before serving. Repeat with the remaining mushrooms.

Fillings

Hot Spinach Cheese Dip (p. 36)
Spinach Herb Filling (p. 67)
Cheese Puffs (p. 37). Preheat the oven to 400 degrees and bake for 20 minutes until the Cheese Puff filling is puffed and well browned.

Cheese Straws

These tidbits of savory cheese pastry are an appealing, light appetizer to awaken the taste buds for dinner—but they're also great for just plain nibbling.

6	tablespoons butter (¾ stick)
1	cup flour
1	cup grated cheddar cheese (4 ounces)
1	egg yolk
2	teaspoons water

Cut the butter into the flour until it is finely distributed throughout. (Use a food processor, pastry blender or two knives.) Stir in the grated cheese. Mix the egg yolk and water and stir into the flour mixture. Process or knead lightly to form a smooth dough. Wrap the dough in plastic wrap and chill for at least 1 hour before rolling it out. The dough can be frozen at this point, then thawed and baked later.

Preheat oven to 375 degrees.

Roll out the dough to about ¼-inch thickness and cut it into ¼-inch-wide strips about 4 inches long. Place the strips on an ungreased baking sheet. Bake for 12 to 15 minutes until lightly brown. Makes about 6 dozen straws.

Idea: To make cheese "coins," shape the dough into 2 cylinders about 2 inches in diameter. When chilled, cut the dough into ¼-inch slices and place on an ungreased baking sheet. Sprinkle the cheese "coins" with caraway seeds, sesame seeds or garlic salt, if desired, lightly pressing the seeds or seasonings into the dough. Bake as for Cheese Straws. Makes about 3 dozen coins.

Chicken Parmesan Drumettes

These miniature chicken drumsticks can be a real party pleaser when dressed up with Paper Frills (p. 155) or a real family pleaser when served as a wholesome snack.

24	**chicken wings**
1	**recipe *Parmesan Bread Crumbs (p. 20)***
$^{1}/_{2}$	**cup butter (1 stick), melted**

Preheat oven to 375 degrees.

Cut the chicken wings apart at the joint to make three pieces.
Discard the wing-tip pieces.

Place the Parmesan Bread Crumbs in a large bowl. Pour the melted butter into a smaller bowl. Dip the chicken pieces into the melted butter, then into the Parmesan Bread Crumbs. Coat them well. Arrange the chicken pieces in a single layer in a shallow baking pan. Bake for 25 minutes or until golden brown. For more even browning, turn the chicken over after 15 minutes of baking. Makes 48 drumettes.

Bread-ahead Chicken Drumettes
If you prefer fried chicken, cut 24 chicken wings as for Chicken Parmesan Drumettes (see above). Follow the recipe for Bread-ahead Fried Chicken (p. 56) for coating the Drumettes. Fry the drumettes for 8 to 10 minutes.

 Everyday Hint: Freezer frost and freezer burn form when air (moisture) is trapped between the food and the container. Both will affect the quality as well as the flavor of frozen foods. When freezing chicken or other foods in a plastic bag, insert a straw just before sealing and suck out the excess air.

Chicken Nuggets

This popular and nourishing snack is also a satisfying, light supper. Whether you choose to bake or fry them, Chicken Nuggets are a fun-to-eat finger food that will disappear very quickly.

8   **boneless, skinless chicken breasts, or other chicken pieces**
1   **recipe *Bread-ahead Fried Chicken coating (p. 56)***

Cut the chicken meat into bite-sized pieces. (Each breast makes 6 to 8 nuggets.) Follow the coating and frying directions for Bread-ahead Fried Chicken, except reduce the frying time to 8 to 10 minutes. Makes 48 to 64 nuggets.

Chicken Parmesan Nuggets

Instead of frying the Chicken Nuggets, coat them with butter and Parmesan Bread Crumbs as described in the Chicken Parmesan Drumettes recipe (p. 42). Bake the nuggets for 20 to 25 minutes or until they are golden brown.

Dipping sauces for Bread-ahead Chicken Nuggets and Drumettes are easy to make and add to the fun of eating these chicken snacks. Any of the salad dressings (p. 88) are great for dips and so are the suggestions listed below. Or be creative and make your own flavor combinations.

Barbecue Sauce: You can make your own, but store-bought is fast and tastes just fine.

Orange Marmalade with Horseradish: Start by mixing ½ cup marmalade with 1 teaspoon horseradish, or more to taste.

Herb Mayonnaise (p. 87): This is a super dip all by itself, but you can vary it with a pinch of curry powder or a spoonful of chutney if you like.

Sweet-and-Sour Sauce: The store-bought version is the quickest and easiest. Look for this sauce in the Oriental section of your grocery store or make your own sauce with apricot preserves mixed with a splash of cider vinegar.

Reuben Caraway Kraut Sandwiches

When friends drop by and there are hearty appetites to feed, mouth-watering Reuben Sandwiches are a fast and filling feast that won't leave you stuck in the kitchen. They're especially delicious made with Caraway Kraut—and don't forget the dill pickle!

8	slices rye or pumpernickel bread
	butter, softened
1/4	pound Swiss cheese, sliced
1	recipe *Caraway Kraut (see below)*
3/4	pound lean corned beef, thinly sliced

For each sandwich, butter one side of each slice of bread. Place one slice buttered-side down on a piece of wax paper. Place the Swiss cheese on the bread. Spread Caraway Kraut on the cheese. Stack corned beef on the Kraut and top with the other piece of bread, buttered side up. Press the sandwich together for more even cooking. (The sandwiches can be made ahead to this point.)

In a hot skillet, electric frypan or griddle, cook the sandwiches on each side over medium heat for several minutes until the bread is toasted and the cheese melts. Cut the sandwiches in halves or quarters and serve with a dill pickle. Makes 4 sandwiches.

Idea: Make tiny Reuben Caraway Kraut Sandwiches on small party rye or pumpernickel bread for lighter snacks.

Caraway Kraut

1	pound sauerkraut
1/2	cup sour cream
2	tablespoons mayonnaise
1	small clove garlic, finely minced
1/2	teaspoon caraway seeds

Rinse the sauerkraut under running water and squeeze it dry. In a bowl, mix together the sour cream, mayonnaise, garlic and caraway seeds, then stir in the sauerkraut. Refrigerate the mixture for about 1 hour to allow the flavors to develop and blend.

Quick Pizza

The ease in making this thin, crispy crust means you can enjoy homemade pizza in the same time it takes to order it.

1	recipe *Homemade Biscuits (p. 110)*
1½	cups pizza sauce (14-oz. jar) or *Homemade Tomato Sauce (p. 101)*
	toppings of your choice (sautéd mushrooms, peppers or onions, pepperoni, cooked sausage or beef, sliced meatballs, etc.)
2	cups grated mozzarella cheese (8 ounces)

Preheat oven to 425 degrees.

Make the Homemade Biscuit recipe, except after kneading the dough, divide it in half. With a rolling pin, roll each half into an 11-inch circle or a rectangle. Place each circle on an ungreased cookie sheet and crimp the edges to form a small ridge for the crust.

Spread the sauce over the surface of the dough. Evenly distribute your choice of toppings over the sauce and sprinkle the mozzarella cheese over the toppings.

Place the baking sheet on the lowest rack of the oven and bake for 12 to 15 minutes or until the cheese is melted and lightly browned. Serve immediately. Makes 2 11-inch or 4 8-inch pizzas.

Idea: Make tiny individual pizza snacks by thinly rolling out the dough and cutting it with a round cutter.

Fried Pasta

When you've got the munchies, crunchy, spiral-shaped pasta hits the spot. Sprinkle it with your favorite flavors—salty, spicy or sweet.

2	cups (or more) uncooked spiral-shaped pasta (spirelli, fusilli, etc.)
	vegetable oil
	garlic salt, seasoned salt or other seasonings

Cook the pasta according to the package directions until it is just tender. Drain and rinse under cold water. Drain the pasta again and pat it dry to remove any excess moisture.

In a frying pan, electric skillet or fryer, heat the oil to 375 degrees. Fry the spirals, small amounts at a time, until they are lightly browned.

Drain the pasta on paper towels, sprinkle it with garlic salt or other seasonings and transfer to a serving bowl. Makes about 3 cups.

Idea: For a sweet treat, sprinkle the fried pasta with sifted confectioner's sugar or cinnamon sugar.

Idea: For variety, use several shapes of pasta, such as farfalle (bows), ruote (cartwheels), conchiglie (shells) or rotelle (corkscrews).

Toasted Pecans

The only problem with making these yummy morsels is that once you start eating them, you can't stop. I make up a double batch, store them in a jar in the refrigerator and have them handy to use in any recipes calling for nuts.

2	**cups pecan halves**
2	**tablespoons butter, cut into small pieces**
1	**teaspoon coarse salt (approx.)**

Preheat oven to 300 degrees.

Place the pecans in a shallow baking dish and top with the butter. Roast them for about 20 minutes, stirring occasionally for more even toasting. Remove the pecans from the oven, drain on paper towels and sprinkle them with salt. Serve warm.

To microwave: Following the same procedure, microwave the nuts on high power for 6 minutes, stirring every minute for more even toasting.

Idea: Instead of salt, sprinkle the hot pecans with seasoned salt.

 Everyday Hint: The flavor of nuts is improved if they are toasted. For added flavor, substitute toasted nuts in any recipe calling for nuts. Some nuts such as almonds or pine nuts and also chopped nuts, toast much more quickly than others, so start checking the nuts after the first 5 minutes of toasting so they don't burn.

 Everyday Hint: Coarse (Kosher) salt can be found in most grocery stores with specialty or ethnic foods. The difference in flavor is worth the search.

Nutty Caramel Corn

You don't need a candy thermometer to make this never-fail caramel popcorn. It's so scrumptious you won't want to share it—but if you can force yourself, it makes a great gift.

16	cups popped popcorn (4 quarts)
2	cups nuts (almonds, pecans, peanuts)
1	cup brown sugar
1/2	cup butter (1 stick)
1/2	cup light corn syrup
1	teaspoon vanilla
1/2	teaspoon baking soda

Preheat oven to 250 degrees.

Coat a large roasting pan and two large spoons with cooking oil spray (or grease them) so the caramel won't stick to them. Stir the popped corn and nuts in the pan and set aside.

In a saucepan, stir together the brown sugar, butter and corn syrup. Over medium heat, stirring constantly, bring the mixture to a boil. Without stirring, continue to boil for 5 minutes. Remove the pan from the heat and stir in the vanilla and baking soda. Pour the caramel over the popcorn and nuts, stirring to coat well.

Bake for 45 minutes, stirring every 15 minutes for even baking and coating of caramel. Remove from the oven and turn the popcorn out onto wax paper to cool. Break apart and store in an airtight container (if there's any left to store!). Makes about 4 quarts.

Tropical Caramel Popcorn

For a truly exotic treat, make caramel corn (see above) with macadamia nuts and coconut (3 1/2-oz. can). Substitute 2 tablespoons rum for the vanilla if you like.

 Everyday Hint: For easy clean-up, coat cooking and stirring utensils with cooking spray or oil when making caramel or other "sticky" recipes.

Main Dishes

I think one of the most challenging things to do on an everyday basis is to figure out new and different ways to make meal time interesting and exciting. Even if we had lots of time, an unlimited budget and a grocery store next door—it would still be a chore.

That's why I've included fast and easy ways to make all-time favorites such as Chicken Pot Pie (p. 52) and Lasagna (p. 70). Don't pass up the chance to change the pace of routine meals with these satisfying chicken or pasta variations. You'll also find simplified versions of classic recipes—such as Chicken Cordon Bleu in Puff Pastry (p. 50), Beef Wellington (p. 64) and Beef Stroganoff (p. 63)—that are perfect for special occasions.

Chicken Cordon Bleu in Puff Pastry

In French, Cordon Bleu means "blue ribbon" and your guests will think you deserve one after you serve this show-stopping entrée. With frozen puff pastry this dish is a no-fuss pleasure to make. It freezes beautifully, so make plenty. For a special treat, serve with Blender Hollandaise Sauce (p. 66).

4	single chicken breasts, skinless and boneless
1	tablespoon butter
1	tablespoon oil
1	recipe *Duxelles (p. 65)*, optional
8	slices cooked ham, about ⅛ inch thick
4	slices Swiss cheese, about ⅛ inch thick
1	10-oz. package frozen puff pastry patty shells, thawed, or frozen puff pastry sheets, thawed
	Blender Hollandaise Sauce (p. 66), optional

Pat the chicken dry with paper towels. In a skillet over medium-high heat, heat the butter and oil. Add the chicken breasts and sear for 20 seconds on each side, but do not cook. Remove from the skillet and set aside to cool completely.

Make Duxelles and set aside to cool.

Cut the ham and cheese slices about the size of the chicken breasts.

Preheat oven to 425 degrees.

Roll out 4 patty shells into 7-inch circles. In the center of the pastry, place a piece of ham. Cover with 1 tablespoon Duxelles. Place the chicken breast on top of the Duxelles. On the chicken breast, spread more Duxelles, a slice of cheese, then another piece of ham. Lift the pastry over the sides of the chicken and ham and make pleat-like folds around the top. The pastry should not cover the top completely.

Roll out the 2 remaining patty shells and cut 2 pastry "lids" out of each shell, large enough to cover the top of pleated pastry. Moisten the edges of each pastry lid and place on top of the chicken-filled pastry. Press gently to seal. (These can be made a day ahead, wrapped in plastic wrap and refrigerated until baking time.)

Place the chicken-filled pastries on an ungreased baking sheet. Bake for 20 to 25 minutes until the pastry is puffed and golden.

To freeze, bake as directed and cool on a cooling rack. Wrap each chicken-filled pastry in plastic wrap. To reheat, place frozen Chicken Cordon Bleu on baking sheet and bake in a preheated 375 degree oven for 30 to 35 minutes or until a skewer or cake tester placed through the center is hot. Makes 4 servings.

Idea: Instead of Duxelles use Spinach Herb Filling (p. 67) with the Chicken Cordon Bleu.

Chicken Rollups

This is a real family-pleaser that takes just minutes in a microwave and only a little longer in a conventional oven. When chicken breasts are on sale, stock your freezer with rollups made with a variety of fillings.

¹/₄	**cup butter (¹/₂ stick), melted**
4	**single chicken breasts, skinless and boneless**
4	**thin slices ham**
4	**thin slices cheese**
1	**cup *Seasoned Bread Crumbs (p. 20)* or other coating**

Preheat oven to 350 degrees.

Melt the butter in a baking dish and set aside. Place a chicken breast, skinned side down, between 2 pieces of plastic wrap. Lightly pound it to flatten the meat for more even cooking.

Remove the top piece of plastic wrap. Place a slice of ham and a slice of cheese on the breast. Starting at the narrow end, tightly roll up the chicken breast.

Coat the rolled breast in the melted butter, then in the Seasoned Bread Crumbs. Repeat with remaining ingredients. (The rollups can be prepared ahead to this point and frozen individually for future use.) Arrange in a baking dish and bake for 35 minutes.

To microwave: In a microwave-safe baking dish, arrange the rollups to form a hollow circle pattern. (This is the best way to place food for even cooking in a microwave oven.) Loosely cover the chicken with wax paper. Microwave on high power for 6 minutes, rotating the dish after 3 minutes. Allow 5 minutes standing time before serving. Makes 4 servings.

Idea: Try other fillings for Chicken Rollups. Before rolling, fill each chicken breast with any of the following:
> 1 tablespoon Herb Butter (p. 18)
> 2 tablespoons Herb Cheese (p. 24)
> 2 tablespoons Spinach Herb Filling (p. 67)

Chicken Pot Pie

This flavorful dish is comfort food at its best when dressed up with a golden puff pastry dome. I like to double or triple the chicken recipe, freeze in individual or family-sized portions and then thaw and cover with puff pastry, pie dough or biscuits before baking.

3	pounds chicken pieces
3	cups chicken broth
1/2	cup chopped onion
1	cup diced celery
6	tablespoons *Herb Butter (p. 18)* or butter, softened
6	tablespoons flour
1	cup heavy cream
1/4	teaspoon pepper
1	10-oz. package frozen mixed vegetables

Simmer the chicken pieces, broth, onion and celery in a covered pot until the chicken is tender, about 30 minutes. Remove the chicken and set aside. When cool enough to handle, skin and bone the chicken and cut it into bite-sized pieces. If desired, skim the chicken fat off the surface of the broth.

To make the sauce, boil the broth until it is reduced to 3 cups. Mix the butter and flour into a paste. Rapidly stir the paste into the boiling broth. Lower the heat to medium and continue to cook, stirring constantly, for a few minutes until the broth thickens. Stir in the cream, add the pepper and simmer, stirring constantly, for several more minutes.

Preheat oven to 425 degrees.

Divide the chicken and vegetables among 6 ovenproof serving bowls. Ladle in the sauce. Top with Puff Pastry Dome (see opposite) or place the chicken, vegetables and sauce in an ovenproof casserole dish. Top with Homemade Biscuits (p. 110) or Drop Biscuits (p. 111).

Bake for 20 minutes or until the pastry or biscuits are golden brown. Makes 6 servings.

 Everyday Hint: For a quick way to thicken a broth or gravy and avoid lumps, too, mix equal portions of flour and butter to form a paste. For each cup of liquid use 2 tablespoons of both butter and flour. Drop the paste into the boiling liquid and stir vigorously until the broth thickens.

Puff Pastry Dome

You can turn your anyday casserole into an everyday gourmet wonder just by topping it with this savory puff pastry dome.

1   **10-oz. package frozen puff pastry patty shells or puff pastry sheets, thawed**
         garlic or herb salt, optional
1   **egg yolk, slightly beaten with 1 teaspoon water for pastry glaze**

Preheat oven to 450 degrees.

Use 6 patty shells or cut the puff pastry into 6 pieces. With a rolling pin, roll the pastry 2 inches wider than the rim of the serving bowl. Sprinkle with garlic or herb salt if desired and pat into the pastry. Brush the pastry with the beaten egg yolk and place, egg side down, over the top of the serving bowl, pressing edges firmly against the sides of the bowl. Be careful not to pierce holes in the pastry or it won't puff. (You can make the pot pie ahead to this point, cover it with plastic and refrigerate until baking time.) Brush egg yolk over the top of the pastry just before baking for a golden crust.

Bake for 20 minutes until the pastry dome is puffed and golden brown.

Chicken à la King

Prepare a double batch of the Chicken Pot Pie (see opposite) without the mixed vegetables and keep it on hand to make this fast and flavorful dish.

1   **recipe *Chicken Pot Pie (p. 52)*, except omit frozen vegetables**
1   **6-oz. can sliced mushrooms, drained**
1   **4-oz. jar sliced pimiento, drained**
1   **cup frozen peas**

Cook the chicken and make the sauce according to the directions for the Chicken Pot Pie recipe. After the sauce has simmered for a few minutes, stir in the chicken pieces, mushrooms, pimiento and frozen peas. Cook over low heat for 3 to 4 minutes.

Serve Chicken à la King in baked patty shells or over Homemade Biscuits (p. 110), toast, rice or noodles. Makes 6 servings.

Chicken Divan

Here's a great way to make your extra chicken or turkey into a delicious meal that no one would ever call "leftovers."

1	recipe *Chicken Pot Pie (p. 52)*, except omit frozen vegetables
2	cups grated cheddar cheese (8 ounces)
2	10-oz. packages frozen broccoli spears, or 2 bunches fresh broccoli

Cook the chicken and make the sauce according to directions for the Chicken Pot Pie recipe, except slice the reserved chicken instead of cutting it into bite-sized pieces. Stir the cheddar cheese into the hot sauce until the cheese is melted. Cook and drain the broccoli and arrange in a large baking pan or individual ovenproof dishes. Lay the chicken slices over the broccoli and top with the cheese sauce (any extra cheese sauce can be frozen for later use). Bake in a 350 degree oven for 25 minutes or until thoroughly heated. Makes 6 servings.

Chicken and Dumplings

On a cold evening nothing beats the simmered goodness of chicken stew with tasty, tender dumplings.

3 to 4	pounds chicken pieces
8	cups chicken broth
½	cup water
1	recipe *Basic Biscuit Mix (p. 25)*

In a large wide pot, simmer the chicken pieces in the broth until the chicken is tender, about 30 minutes. Remove the chicken and set it aside. When cool enough to handle, skin and bone the chicken and shred or cut it into bite-sized pieces. If desired, skim the chicken fat off the surface of the broth.

Stir the water into the Basic Biscuit Mix and knead as instructed in the Homemade Biscuit recipe (p. 110). Roll the dough out to ⅛-inch thickness and cut into 1-inch squares. Bring the broth to a rolling boil, drop in the dumplings, cover the pot and reduce the heat to simmer. Cook for 10 minutes or until the dumplings are cooked. Overcooking will cause the dumplings to fall apart.

To serve, place the chicken pieces in a bowl and ladle hot broth and dumplings over the chicken. Makes 4 to 6 servings.

Chicken Parmesan

Just add Parmesan cheese to your own homemade Seasoned Bread Crumbs to make this savory coating for oven-baked chicken. It's a real crowd-pleaser.

2	cups *Parmesan Bread Crumbs* (p. 20)
8	large pieces chicken, skinned or unskinned
1/2	cup butter (1 stick), melted

Preheat oven to 375 degrees.

Place the Parmesan Bread Crumbs in a large bowl. Dip the chicken into melted butter, then into the crumb mixture. Be sure to coat the chicken well.

Arrange coated chicken pieces in a single layer in an ungreased shallow baking pan. Bake them for about 45 minutes or until golden brown. For more even browning, turn the chicken over after 30 minutes of baking. Makes 4 servings.

Shrimp in Scampi Sauce

The wonderful aroma of shrimp and garlic will make everyone in your house eager for dinner. Serve with a basket of crusty bread for soaking up every last drop of the delicious sauce.

1 1/2	pounds shrimp, peeled and deveined, or 1 pound frozen, unthawed
8	ounces fresh mushrooms, halved or quartered, optional
1/2	cup *Herb Butter* (p. 18)
1/2	cup *Parmesan Bread Crumbs* (p. 20)

Preheat oven to 425 degrees.

Divide the shrimp and mushrooms among 4 individual ovenproof dishes or place in a large baking dish. Evenly dot the Herb Butter over the shrimp.

Sprinkle the Parmesan Bread Crumbs over the Herb Butter and the shrimp. Bake for 15 to 20 minutes for fresh shrimp, or 20 to 25 minutes for frozen shrimp, or until cooked. Makes 4 main dishes or 6 to 8 appetizers.

 Everyday Hint: Shellfish should not be overcooked or it will become tough and rubbery.

Bread-ahead Fried Chicken

Crispy-fried chicken is an all-American favorite, and when you bread it ahead of time, the coating stays on the chicken instead of falling off in the pan.

3	**pounds chicken pieces**
¼	**cup milk or water**
1	**cup flour**
2	**teaspoons salt**
1	**teaspoon pepper**
	oil for frying

Rinse the chicken pieces and pat them dry. Pour the milk into a large plastic bag. In another plastic (or paper) bag combine the flour, salt and pepper. Shake the chicken in the milk, then in the seasoned flour, coating just a few pieces at a time.

Place the coated chicken on a wire rack on a baking sheet and cover loosely with plastic wrap. Refrigerate overnight or at least several hours so the coating will dry.

In a frying pan, electric skillet or fryer, heat at least 2 inches of oil to 375 degrees (medium-high heat). Fry the chicken a few pieces at a time, turning occasionally, until golden brown. This takes about 20 minutes depending on the size of the chicken pieces. Drain on paper towels and keep warm while frying the remaining pieces. Makes 4 servings.

Lemon Fried Chicken: Dip the chicken in lemon juice instead of milk. Add 1 teaspoon freshly grated lemon rind to the flour mixture before coating the chicken.

Hot 'n Spicy Chicken: Add 1 to 3 teaspoons chili powder, red or cayenne pepper to the flour mixture before coating the chicken.

Finger-lickin' Chicken: Add 2 packages (.07-oz. each) dried Italian salad dressing mix to the flour mixture before coating the chicken.

Everyday Hint: When coating any food, use one hand for dipping the food into the wet ingredient, drop it into the dry coating, then use the other hand for coating it with the dry ingredients. This way you coat the food and not your fingers!

Everyday Hint: To re-use cooking oil, strain the oil through a fine sieve before storing and add some fresh oil before heating again.

Cornish Hens with Savory Apricot Sauce

Cornish hens are just the right size for one hearty appetite or two smaller ones. They're especially tasty when served with this surprisingly savory instead of sweet apricot sauce.

6	**Cornish hens**
2	**tablespoons lemon juice**
¹/₂	**cup** *Herb Butter (p. 18),* **frozen in teaspoon-sized pieces**
1	**recipe** *Savory Apricot Sauce (see below)*

Preheat oven to 375 degrees.

If frozen, thaw the hens in their wrappers. Remove the giblets and rinse the hens inside and out. Dry the inside and outside with paper towels, then sprinkle about 1 teaspoon lemon juice inside each hen. Cross the legs and tie them together at the "ankles" with kitchen string. (Don't use nylon string or it will melt.)

Starting at the neck end, separate the skin from the meat over the breast and thighs with your fingers, being careful not to tear the skin. Slide 4 pieces of frozen Herb Butter under the skin, placing one piece over each thigh and breast. Rub the outside of the skin with softened Herb Butter, if desired.

Place the hens breast side up on a greased rack in a baking pan. Bake for 1 hour. Turn the hens over and bake for 15 more minutes to allow even browning.

To serve, with a sharp knife split hens in half lengthwise through the breast bone and back bone. Arrange on a plate, cut side down. Spoon on the Savory Apricot Sauce (below) and serve with Mini Stuffin' Muffins (p. 119). Makes 6 servings.

Savory Apricot Sauce

1	**17-oz. can apricot halves in syrup**
¹/₄	**cup brown sugar**
1	**tablespoon cornstarch**
1	**clove garlic**
1	**tablespoon lemon juice**
1	**teaspoon Dijon mustard**
¹/₂	**teaspoon Worcestershire sauce**
3	**ounces dried apricots, thinly sliced**
2	**tablespoons** *Herb Butter (p. 18)*

In a blender or food processor, pour in the can of apricots, brown sugar, cornstarch, garlic, lemon juice, mustard and Worcestershire sauce. Blend well. (The sauce can be made ahead to this point.) Pour the mixture into a saucepan. Stir in the sliced dried apricots and bring the mixture to a boil. Cook until thickened. Quickly stir in the Herb Butter. Serve the sauce hot with poultry or pork. Makes about 2 cups.

Medallions of Turkey with Mushroom Tarragon Sauce

Here is a delicately flavored classic dish that's very quick and easy to make. You can even purchase ready-sliced turkey at your supermarket meat counter and make this a rush-hour special.

1½	**pounds breast of turkey, cut into ¼-inch slices**
2	**tablespoons butter**
2	**tablespoons oil**
2	**tablespoons minced onion**
½	**cup dry white wine or dry vermouth**
1	**cup beef broth**
2	**tablespoons *Herb Butter (p. 18)* or butter, softened**
2	**tablespoons flour**
1	**cup heavy cream**
8	**ounces fresh mushrooms, halved or quartered**
1	**teaspoon dried tarragon or 1 tablespoon fresh**

Dry the turkey slices with paper towels. In a large skillet, heat the butter and the oil over medium-high heat. Place several turkey slices in the skillet (do not crowd them) and cook for 1 minute on each side. Transfer the turkey to a plate. Continue until all the turkey is cooked.

Add the onion to the skillet and cook, stirring, for 30 seconds. Turn the heat to high, pour in the wine and beef broth and stir to loosen the drippings on the bottom of the pan.

Bring the mixture to a rolling boil. Mix the Herb Butter and flour together to form a paste. Stirring quickly, drop the paste into the boiling broth and continue to stir for 1 minute until the sauce is very thick. Add the cream and mushrooms, stir and boil for 2 minutes until the sauce has been reduced and thickened slightly.

Turn the heat to low and stir in the tarragon. Return the turkey to the skillet, basting with the sauce. (The dish can be made ahead to this point.) Simmer for a few minutes until the turkey is heated. Makes 4 servings.

Idea: For Medallions of Veal with Mushroom Tarragon Sauce, use veal slices in place of turkey.

Ham and Spinach in Puff Pastry

Layers of ham and spinach wrapped in puff pastry look beautiful on a plate and taste even better. They're perfect for a special brunch and add a festive touch to any dinner.

2	pounds cooked ham, sliced ¼ inch thick
2	tablespoons butter
½	cup chopped onion
2	10-oz. packages frozen chopped spinach, thawed
1	3-oz. package cream cheese, cut into pieces, or ⅓ cup *Herb Cheese (p. 24)*
1	cup grated cheddar cheese (4 ounces)
2	eggs, slightly beaten
1	10-oz. package frozen puff pastry patty shells, thawed

Cut the ham slices into 18 3-inch circles (3 per person). Set aside.

In a skillet over medium-heat, heat the butter. Add the onion and cook until soft. Squeeze the water out of the spinach. Stir the spinach and cream cheese (or Herb Cheese) into the onion until well mixed and the cheese has melted. Remove the pan from the heat. Stir in the cheddar cheese and eggs. Set aside to cool.

With a rolling pin, roll out each patty shell to form an 8-inch circle. Place a piece of ham in the center of the pastry circle. Spread the ham with 2 tablespoons spinach mixture. Top with another ham circle, 2 more tablespoons spinach, then the third piece of ham. Gather the pastry up around the ham and pinch the top together to form a "package." Repeat for the remaining pastry, ham and spinach.

If prepared a day ahead, cover the packages with plastic wrap and refrigerate until baking time.

Preheat oven to 425 degrees.

Place the ham and spinach packages on an ungreased baking sheet and bake for 20 to 25 minutes until the pastry is puffed and golden. Serve alone or with Cheddar Cheese Sauce (p. 107). Makes 6 servings.

A Finished Ham and Spinach in Puff Pastry "Package"

Crispy Pork Loin

Sliced very thin, quick-coated and browned until crispy, this pork loin is full of flavor and takes only a short time to prepare.

1 1/2	pounds lean, boneless pork loin
1/2	cup milk
1/2	cup flour
1	teaspoon salt
1/2	teaspoon pepper
2	tablespoons butter
1	tablespoon oil

Trim the pork loin of any excess fat and cut it into very thin slices (1/4 inch or less). Place the pork in a bowl. Pour in the milk and stir to coat the pork.

Mix together the flour, salt and pepper and spread on a plate or wax paper. Coat each pork slice on both sides with the seasoned flour.

In a large skillet, heat the butter and oil over high heat. Cook the pork, a few pieces at a time, until nicely browned and crisp, about 2 minutes on each side. Makes 4 servings.

Serve the pork with Hot Caramel Apples (p. 134) or Carrots in Caramel Sauce (p. 106) or applesauce.

Pan Gravy

There are many ways to make a flour- and butter-based (roux) sauce or gravy. This is the one I find to be the easiest and fastest. Use any of the variations to fit whatever food you are making (or leftovers you are stretching!). If you have meat drippings, add them for even more flavor and color.

1	cup broth (beef or chicken), or clam juice
2	tablespoons flour
2	tablespoons *Herb Butter (p. 18)* or butter, softened

Bring the liquid to a boil. Mix the flour and Herb Butter together to form a smooth paste. Drop the paste into the boiling liquid, stirring briskly. Reduce the heat and let the gravy cook for a few minutes to thicken. Makes 1 cup.

For a thicker gravy, use 2 tablespoons Herb Butter and 3 tablespoons flour to 1 cup liquid.

Idea: For flavor variation add sautéd onions, sliced mushrooms or Duxelles (p. 65) to the gravy, or substitute up to 1/2 cup wine for the broth.

Pork with Apple Onion Sauce

The down-home flavor of this robust dish evokes comfort with every bite. Its companion is Apple Walnut Stuffing served as Stuffin' Muffins (p. 119).

1½	pounds boneless pork loin
2	tablespoons butter
2	tablespoons oil
1	cup thinly sliced onions
1	cup apple juice
½	cup chicken broth
2	tablespoons *Herb Butter (p. 18)* or butter, softened
2	tablespoons flour

Trim the pork loin of any excess fat and cut into very thin slices (¼ inch or less). Dry the pork slices with paper towels.

In a large skillet, heat the butter and oil over high heat. Place several pork slices in the skillet (do not crowd them) and cook about 2 minutes on each side until the pork is nicely browned. Transfer the pork to a plate. Continue until all the pork is cooked. Lower the heat to medium and add the onions to the skillet. Cook for 3 to 5 minutes, stirring occasionally, until the onions are tender. Add more butter if necessary. On high heat, pour in the apple juice and chicken broth and stir to loosen the drippings on the bottom of the pan. Bring the mixture to a rolling boil. Mix the Herb Butter and flour together to form a paste. Stirring quickly, drop the paste into the boiling broth and continue to stir for a few minutes until the sauce has thickened. Return the pork to the skillet, basting with the sauce. (The dish can be made ahead to this point.) Simmer for a few minutes until the pork is heated. Makes 4 servings.

Apple Walnut Stuffing

8	cups homemade-style bread cut into cubes
½	cup butter (1 stick)
½	cup chopped celery
½	cup chopped onion
2	tablespoons chopped parsley
¼	teaspoon pepper
1	egg, slightly beaten
¼	cup water
2	apples, cored, peeled and diced
1	cup chopped walnuts

Cut the bread into 1-inch cubes and place in a large bowl. In a skillet, heat the butter. Stir in the celery, onion, parsley and pepper. Cook over medium-low heat until softened but not browned, then stir into the bread cubes. Combine the egg and water, add to the stuffing and mix thoroughly. Fold in the apples and walnuts. Makes 12 muffins or 30 mini-muffins.

Beef Burgundy

This hearty, aromatic stew starts easily on the top of the range before going into the oven for long, slow simmering. It tastes even better the second day, and freezes beautifully.

2	tablespoons oil
2	tablespoons butter
1½	cups chopped onion
1½	cups carrots, cut into chunks
1	pound fresh mushrooms, whole or cut in half
3	pounds boneless lean beef (round, chuck or sirloin tip), cut into 1½-inch cubes
2	cups red Burgundy or other dry red wine
2½	cups beef broth
½	cup *Herb Butter (p. 18)* or butter, softened
½	cup flour
½	teaspoon dried thyme, optional
2	cloves garlic, chopped

Preheat oven to 325 degrees.

In a large skillet, heat the oil and butter over medium-high heat. Cook the onion and carrots for 2 minutes and transfer to a 4-quart ovenproof casserole with a lid. Add the mushrooms to the casserole.

In the skillet, brown the beef cubes on all sides. Do not crowd the pan. Transfer the beef to the casserole.

Over high heat, add the wine and beef broth to the skillet and bring to a boil. Mix together the Herb Butter and flour to make a smooth paste. Drop it into the boiling broth, stirring for several minutes until thickened.

Stir in the thyme and garlic, then pour the sauce over the beef and vegetables in the casserole. Cover and bake for 1½ to 2 hours or until meat is tender when pierced with a fork. Makes 6 to 8 servings.

Idea: Add small whole potatoes (or large chunks) to the casserole during the last hour of cooking. Or make Beef Burgundy Pot Pies: cover individual casseroles of Beef Burgundy with Puff Pastry Dome (p. 53) or Homemade Biscuits (p. 110).

Beef Stroganoff

A rich, tangy, sour-cream flavor highlights this traditional dish. For the smoothest sauce, let the sour cream come to room temperature and stir it in quickly just before serving.

1½	**pounds beef tenderloin or sirloin**
2	**tablespoons butter**
2	**tablespoons oil**
2	**tablespoons minced onion**
½	**cup dry white wine or dry vermouth**
1	**cup beef broth**
4	**tablespoons *Herb Butter (p. 18)* or butter, softened**
4	**tablespoons flour**
8	**ounces fresh mushrooms, thickly sliced**
1	**cup sour cream, room temperature**

Slice the beef into ¼-inch strips about 1 x 4 inches long.

In a large skillet, heat the butter and oil over medium-high heat. Place several beef slices in the skillet (do not crowd them) and cook for 30 seconds on each side. Transfer the beef to a plate. Continue until all the beef is cooked.

Add the onion to the skillet and cook, stirring, for 1 minute. Turn the heat to high, pour in the wine and beef broth and stir to loosen the drippings on the bottom of the pan.

Bring the mixture to a rapid boil. Mix the Herb Butter and flour together to form a paste. Rapidly stir the paste into the boiling broth. Lower the heat to medium, add the mushrooms and continue to stir for about 3 minutes until the sauce is thick. Add the beef to the skillet and heat for about 1 minute. (The stroganoff can be made ahead to this point and reheated before continuing with the recipe.)

Remove the skillet from the heat and quickly stir in the sour cream. Serve immediately over rice or noodles. Makes 4 servings.

Beef Wellington

For show-off occasions this elegant dish will wow company. Although it looks difficult, it's quite simple to make and can be prepared ahead of time. Easy Everyday Béarnaise Sauce (p. 66) is the perfect accompaniment.

1	recipe *Sour Cream Pastry (see opposite)*
1	recipe *Duxelles (see opposite)*
4	fillets of beef tenderloin, cut 1 inch thick
1	tablespoon butter
1	tablespoon oil
1	egg yolk slightly beaten with 1 teaspoon water for pastry glaze

Prepare the pastry and divide it into 4 equal pieces. Shape each piece into a flat circle. Wrap the pastry in plastic wrap and refrigerate for at least 20 minutes before rolling out.

Prepare the Duxelles and set aside to cool.

With a paper towel, pat the fillets dry. In a heavy skillet, heat the butter and oil over medium-high heat. Place the meat in the skillet and sear the fillets (do not cook) for just 20 seconds on each side. Remove from the skillet and set aside to cool completely.

On a lightly floured surface or between 2 pieces of wax paper or plastic wrap, roll out a piece of the chilled dough into a rectangle approximately 2 1/2 times the size of the fillet, about 6 x 8 inches. (Keep the remaining dough refrigerated until ready to roll out.) Trim the dough to make the sides even, saving the scraps. In the center of the pastry, place one-quarter of the mushroom mixture. Pat the fillets dry with paper towels and place a fillet on top of the mushrooms. Fold the two longer sides of the pastry over the fillet and press together gently to seal. Fold the other two sides into the center and seal them. Repeat with the remaining pastry circles and fillets. Turn the pastry packages over, seam side down.

With a small round cutter or knife, cut a 1/2-inch circle through the center of the dough of each pastry, leaving the circles in place. These "vents" allow the steam to escape and keep the dough from cracking and getting soggy. Use the scraps of dough to cut petal shapes and place them around the circles to form flower designs. Cover with plastic wrap and refrigerate until ready to bake. (This dish can be made early in the day to this point.)

Preheat oven to 425 degrees.

Place the Beef Wellingtons on an ungreased baking sheet. Just before baking, brush the top and sides of the dough with the egg yolk glaze. Bake for 15 to 20 minutes or until lightly browned. Serve with Everyday Béarnaise Sauce (p. 66). Makes 4 servings.

Idea: Instead of Sour Cream Pastry, use puff pastry dough to wrap the beef fillets, except do not cut the vent in the dough.

Sour Cream Pastry

2	**cups flour**
1	**teaspoon salt**
$^{1}/_{2}$	**cup butter (1 stick)**
1	**egg**
$^{1}/_{4}$	**cup sour cream**

Stir together the flour and salt. Using a food processor, pastry blender or two knives, cut in the butter until it is finely distributed throughout the flour. Mix together the egg and sour cream and stir into the flour. Turn the dough out onto a lightly floured surface and press it together. Knead the dough just until it holds together. Refrigerate the dough for at least 20 minutes before rolling out.

 Everyday Hint: Roll out pie or pastry dough between two pieces of plastic wrap or wax paper to keep it from sticking to the rolling pin and surface. This also makes it easier to transfer the dough to a pie plate or baking dish.

Duxelles (Mushroom Paste)

2	**tablespoons butter**
2	**tablespoons finely minced onion**
8	**ounces fresh mushrooms, finely minced**
	salt and pepper

In a skillet over medium-high heat, heat the butter and cook the onion until soft. Add the mushrooms and stir over high heat until the liquid has evaporated and the mixture is very dry. Season with salt and pepper. Makes 1 cup.

Blender Hollandaise Sauce

If just the thought of attempting a classic sauce puts you in a tizzy, try this blender version. Spare yourself last-minute frenzy with easy, make-ahead Hollandaise. This delicate sauce classically graces vegetables or meat dishes.

2	egg yolks, room temperature
1	tablespoon warm water
3/4	cup butter (1 1/2 sticks), melted and bubbling hot
1	tablespoon lemon juice
1/4	teaspoon Worcestershire sauce
	salt, if needed

Put the egg yolks and warm water in a blender or food processor and blend for 1 minute. With the blender running, pour in the hot butter in a thin, steady stream, then add the lemon juice and Worcestershire sauce. Serve immediately or keep warm in a double boiler over warm, not boiling, water. If the sauce gets too thick add warm water a teaspoon at a time. Makes 1 cup.

Idea: Leftover sauce can be refrigerated or frozen and warmed slowly over warm water.

Everyday Béarnaise Sauce

The magnificent flavor of classic Béarnaise Sauce comes from the perfect reduction of herbs and shallots in wine before being added to Hollandaise Sauce. This everyday version is equally delicious and far easier. It's a perfect companion to beef and veal dishes.

1	recipe *Blender Hollandaise Sauce (see above),* except substitute *Herb Butter (p. 18)* for the butter
1	teaspoon dried tarragon

Follow the instructions for Blender Hollandaise Sauce, using hot Herb Butter. Add the tarragon and blend. Makes 1 cup.

Everyday Hint: Make Blender Hollandaise or Everyday Béarnaise Sauce up to an hour before serving and store in a wide-mouthed Thermos that has been warmed with hot water and emptied before adding the sauce.

Fillet of Flounder Pinwheels

Even people who aren't crazy about fish love the flavor of these delicious pinwheels.

4 to 6   large flounder fillets, boneless and skinless
1   recipe *Spinach Herb Filling (see below)*

Preheat oven to 350 degrees.

Pat each fillet dry and lay flat with the darker or skinned side up. Divide and spread the Spinach Herb Filling over each fillet.

Starting at the narrow end, roll up each fillet. Secure with a toothpick if necessary. Place the fillets in a lightly buttered baking dish and cover with buttered wax paper. Bake for 15 to 20 minutes until the fish is cooked throughout.

Idea: For a crisp coating, roll the fish pinwheels in melted butter, then in Seasoned Bread Crumbs (p. 20). Bake uncovered. Makes 4 to 6 servings.

Spinach Herb Filling

Use this versatile filling with fish or poultry—or to stuff tomatoes or mushrooms.

1   10-oz. package frozen chopped spinach, thawed
2   tablespoons butter
¹/₂   cup chopped onion
1   cup *Herb Cheese (p. 24)*

Squeeze the water out of the spinach. In a skillet over medium heat, heat the butter and cook the onion until softened. Add the spinach and Herb Cheese, stirring until well blended. Cool slightly before using. Makes about 1 ¹/₂ cups.

Veal Oscar

This classic dish reaches perfection with its sublime blend of wonderful flavors. It's a dish that's fit for your most prestigious occasions.

1½	pounds veal scallops cut into slices ⅛ inch thick
½	cup flour
2	tablespoons butter
2	tablespoons oil
¼	cup white wine or dry vermouth
½	cup beef broth
4	pieces Alaskan crab meat (legs or claws), warmed in butter
8	asparagus spears, cooked
1	recipe *Everyday Béarnaise Sauce (p. 66)*

Trim all the visible fat and tendons from the veal. Lightly coat each scallop with flour, shaking off the excess.

In a large skillet, heat the butter and oil over medium-high heat. Place several veal scallops in the skillet (do not crowd them) and cook for 30 to 45 seconds on each side. Do not overcook them. Transfer the veal to a plate. Continue until all the veal is cooked. Add more butter if needed.

Pour the fat out of the skillet. Turn the heat to high and pour in the wine and beef broth, stirring to loosen the drippings on the bottom of the pan. Boil the liquid until it is reduced by half. Remove the pan from the heat and return the veal to the skillet. Cover the pan and set it aside until ready to serve.

To serve, divide the veal scallops among 4 warmed plates, arranging the veal so it is in an overlapping row. Center 1 piece of crab meat on the veal and place 1 asparagus spear on each side of the crab meat on top of the veal. Top with 2 to 3 tablespoons Everyday Béarnaise Sauce. Place the remaining sauce in a sauce bowl. Makes 4 servings.

Idea: To make Veal-less Oscar, substitute turkey breast for veal. It's much less costly and tastes divine.

Pasta Primavera

This light-and-easy dish is a great way to stretch your budget but not your waistline. Use any veggies you have on hand. It's my favorite way to clean out the vegetable drawer.

8	ounces spaghetti or other dried pasta
1/4	cup oil
1	medium onion, sliced
2	cloves garlic, minced
4	ounces fresh mushrooms, quartered
4	cups raw vegetables, sliced or cut into bite-sized pieces (broccoli florets, zucchini, yellow squash, carrots, snow peas, peppers, etc.)
1/2	cup chicken broth
2	tablespoons lemon juice
1/2	teaspoon salt
1/4	teaspoon pepper
1/2	cup grated Parmesan or Romano cheese

Cook the pasta according to package directions just until tender (*al dente*). Drain well.

While the pasta is cooking, in a large skillet heat the oil over medium-high heat. Stir in the onion, garlic and mushrooms and cook, stirring, for 1 minute. Add the other vegetables and stir-fry for just 2 minutes, continuously tossing them with two spoons or spatulas.

Add the chicken broth, lemon juice, salt and pepper. Cook just a few minutes more until the vegetables are tender-crisp and some of the liquid has evaporated. Toss the vegetables with the hot spaghetti and sprinkle with the cheese. Makes 2 large main dishes or 4 to 6 side dishes.

 Everyday Hint: When stir-frying vegetables, the oil should be hot and the vegetables cut into small pieces. Vary the shapes and colors of the vegetables for eye appeal. Cut the vegetables that take longer to cook into smaller pieces and those that cook more quickly into larger pieces. This way all the vegetables will finish cooking at the same time.

Lasagna

This family favorite is a snap to make and there's no need to precook the lasagna noodles beforehand—they cook in the oven. Make a double batch, let it cool, then cut it into individual serving portions before freezing.

1	**pound ground meat**
3	**cups** *Homemade Tomato Sauce (p. 101)* **or spaghetti sauce**
1	**recipe** *Ricotta Filling (p. 71)*
8	**ounces dried lasagna noodles (9 noodles)**
	mozzarella and Parmesan cheese for topping

Preheat oven to 350 degrees.

In a skillet over medium heat, cook the ground meat until it is just lightly browned. Drain the meat well and stir into the Homemade Tomato Sauce.

In an 8 x 12-inch glass baking dish, spread ½ cup sauce. Place 3 *uncooked* lasagna noodles side by side over the sauce. Spread ⅓ of the Ricotta Filling over the noodles. Spread 1 cup sauce over the filling. Repeat the layers with the remaining ingredients, ending with the sauce.

Cover the lasagna tightly with aluminum foil and bake it for 1 hour. Remove the foil, top with additional cheese and bake for 5 more minutes until the cheese has melted. Remove the lasagna from the oven and allow it to stand for at least 10 minutes before cutting. This allows it to cool slightly so the layers will stay intact when served.

To make microwave lasagna: Break up the ground meat and place it in a plastic colander. Place the colander over a glass bowl. Microwave meat on high for 6 minutes, stirring every 2 minutes. Discard drippings and stir the meat into the tomato sauce.

Assemble the lasagna in a glass baking dish and microwave uncovered on medium (50%) power for 35 minutes, rotating the dish every 10 minutes. Top with cheese and microwave on high (100%) power for 2 to 3 minutes until the cheese has melted. Allow lasagna to stand for at least 10 minutes before cutting. Makes 6 servings.

Lasagna Pinwheels

Here's an easy way to give lasagna an appetizing new look. Stuff the pasta with either Ricotta or Florentine fillings for two completely different-tasting meals.

8	ounces lasagna (about 9 pieces)
1	recipe *Ricotta Filling (see below)*
	or 1 recipe *Florentine Filling (see below)*
3 to 4	cups *Homemade Tomato Sauce (p. 101)*
	or 32-oz. jar ready-made spaghetti sauce

Preheat oven to 350 degrees.

Cook lasagna according to package directions. Drain well, rinse with cold water and pat dry with towels. Spoon about ¹/₃ cup filling mixture onto each piece of lasagna, leaving 1 inch on one end uncovered. Starting at the opposite end, roll up the filled lasagna into a pinwheel. Repeat with the remaining lasagna.

In a large baking pan or individual ovenproof baking dishes, spoon in enough sauce to cover the bottom. Arrange the pinwheels, seam side down, over the sauce and spoon the remaining sauce over the pinwheels. Cover with aluminum foil and bake for 20 minutes. Remove the aluminum foil and continue baking for 15 minutes or until the pinwheels are heated all the way through. Makes 9 pinwheels. Use 2 to 3 per serving.

Ricotta Filling

3	cups ricotta cheese (24 ounces)
¹/₂	cup grated mozzarella cheese (2 ounces)
¹/₂	cup grated Parmesan cheese
2	eggs, lightly beaten
1	tablespoon chopped parsley
1¹/₂	teaspoons salt

In a large bowl, combine the ricotta, mozzarella and Parmesan cheese with the eggs, parsley and salt.

Florentine Filling

2	cups ricotta cheese
1	cup *Herb Cheese (p. 24)*, softened
2	10-oz. packages frozen chopped spinach, thawed

In a large bowl, combine the ricotta and Herb Cheese. Squeeze the water out of the spinach and stir into the cheese mixture.

Idea: Ricotta or Florentine Filling may be used to fill lasagna, manicotti, pasta shells, ravioli, etc.

Fettuccine Alfredo

With the everyday basic Alfredo Sauce (p. 23) on hand, you can have dinner ready in the time it takes to cook the pasta!

8	**ounces fettuccine or other dried pasta**
¹/₂	**cup *Alfredo Sauce (p. 23)*, room temperature**

Cook the fettuccine according to package directions until just tender (*al dente*). Drain well. Toss the fettuccine with the Alfredo Sauce, coating the pasta evenly. Makes 2 large main dishes or 4 to 6 side dishes.

Fettuccine Alfredo Primavera

Combining tender-crisp, stir-fried vegetables with Alfredo Sauce (p. 23) adds special crunch and flavor and makes this fettuccine a complete one-dish meal.

8	**ounces fettuccine or other dried pasta**
¹/₄	**cup oil**
	onion, garlic, mushrooms and vegetables, as for *Pasta Primavera (p. 69)*
¹/₂	**cup *Alfredo Sauce (p. 23)*, room temperature**

Cook the fettuccine according to package directions until just tender (*al dente*). Drain well. While the fettuccine is cooking, stir-fry the onion, garlic, mushrooms and other vegetables as directed in the Pasta Primavera recipe. Toss the fettuccine with the Alfredo Sauce, coating the pasta evenly. Lightly toss the tender-crisp vegetables with the fettuccine. Makes 2 large main dishes or 4 to 6 side dishes.

Everyday Hint: Pasta or noodles can be cooked up to a day ahead. Cook the pasta until just tender (*al dente*), drain and toss with a few tablespoons of oil or butter to keep it from sticking together. Cover and refrigerate. Before serving, drop pasta in boiling water for 1 to 2 minutes to reheat, or cover with plastic wrap and microwave on high power for 2 to 3 minutes or until hot.

Straw and Hay Pasta

Italians call this delightful green and white pasta combination "paglia e fieno" because the colors resemble straw and hay. The addition of cooked ham and peas gives extra flavor and eye appeal.

4	ounces fettuccine or other dried pasta
4	ounces spinach fettuccine or other dried spinach pasta
$\frac{1}{2}$	cup *Alfredo Sauce (p. 23)*, room temperature
1	10-oz. package frozen peas, cooked and drained
1	cup diced cooked ham, or crisp bacon, crumbled

Cook the fettuccine according to package directions until just tender (*al dente*). Drain well. Toss the fettuccine with the Alfredo Sauce, coating the pasta evenly. Lightly toss the peas and ham with the fettuccine. Makes 2 large main dishes or 4 to 6 side dishes.

Fettuccine with Pesto Cream Sauce

The rich Alfredo flavor is complemented here by the delicate essence of basil. And easy-to-make basil oil gives you pesto sauce pronto!

8	ounces fettuccine or other dried pasta
$\frac{1}{2}$	cup *Alfredo Sauce (p. 23)*, room temperature
1	small clove garlic, finely minced
3 to 4	tablespoons *Basil Oil (see below)*, or ready-made pesto sauce
2	tablespoons toasted pine nuts, optional

Cook the fettuccine according to package directions until just tender (*al dente*). Drain well. In a bowl, beat together the Alfredo Sauce, garlic and Basil Oil. Toss the fettuccine with the sauce, coating the pasta evenly. Before serving, sprinkle toasted pine nuts over the fettuccine. Makes 2 large main dishes or 4 to 6 side dishes.

Basil Oil
In a blender or food processor, puree 2 cups packed fresh basil leaves and $\frac{1}{3}$ cup flavorless vegetable oil. Store in freezer. Makes $\frac{1}{2}$ cup.

Oven-baked Pasta

This version of the traditional "pasta al forno," or pasta baked in the oven—here it's formed in a pan—gives you nice, neat portions to serve with tomato sauce or a bread-crumb topping.

8	ounces spaghetti
1	small clove garlic, minced, optional
1/2	cup *Alfredo Sauce (p. 23)*, room temperature
2	eggs, slightly beaten

Preheat oven to 375 degrees.

Cook the spaghetti according to package directions, undercooking it slightly. Drain well.

While the spaghetti is cooking, butter (or spray with cooking oil) an 8- or 9-inch cake pan. Beat the garlic into the Alfredo Sauce, then beat in the eggs gradually, making sure that they are incorporated into the sauce.

Toss the hot spaghetti with the sauce mixture, coating the pasta evenly. Pour into the prepared cake pan and cover with buttered wax paper or aluminum foil, pressing down slightly to level the "cake."

Bake in a water bath by placing the cake pan in another larger pan in the oven. Pour boiling water into the larger pan to reach halfway up the sides of the cake pan. Bake for 15 minutes.

To microwave: Place the spaghetti mixture in a buttered microwave-safe baking dish. Cover with buttered wax paper. Microwave on high (100%) power for 5 minutes, rotating the dish halfway through the cooking time. Allow to stand for 5 minutes before unmolding.

To serve, invert the spaghetti onto a serving dish and cut into wedges or squares. Sprinkle the top with toasted Seasoned Bread Crumbs (p. 20) or serve with Homemade Tomato Sauce (p. 101). Makes 4 to 6 servings.

Idea: For an elegant presentation, bake the pasta in a ring mold, unmold onto a serving platter and fill the center with stir-fried vegetables or your favorite meat or seafood casserole recipe.

 Everyday Hint: Baking food in a water bath allows it to cook gently and evenly without browning or forming a crust. For safety's sake, always place the larger pan in the oven first and then pour the hot water into it.

Linguine with Shrimp and Mushrooms

Shrimp and mushrooms are an inviting combination, especially when served on a bed of pasta tossed in garlic and Alfredo Sauce (p. 23).

1	pound linguine or other dried pasta
1	cup *Alfredo Sauce (p. 23)*, room temperature
1	small clove garlic, minced
2	tablespoons butter
2	tablespoons oil or *Garlic Oil (p. 22)*
1	pound shrimp, peeled and deveined, or frozen shrimp
8	ounces fresh mushrooms, halved or quartered

Cook pasta according to package directions or until just tender (*al dente*). Drain well. Beat the Alfredo Sauce and minced garlic together. Toss the linguine with the Alfredo Sauce, coating the pasta evenly.

While the pasta is cooking, heat the butter and oil in a large skillet over medium-high heat. Cook the shrimp, stirring frequently, for 2 to 3 minutes or just until cooked. Remove the shrimp from the skillet and set aside. If needed, heat another tablespoon butter in the skillet. Add the mushrooms and cook for 1 to 2 minutes, continuing to stir. Return the shrimp to the skillet and keep warm until ready to serve.

On each serving dish arrange the pasta in the shape of a "nest." Spoon the shrimp and mushrooms into the center of each nest. Makes 4 servings.

 Everyday Hint: When cutting shrimp into smaller pieces, instead of chopping them, slice the shrimp in half lengthwise through the back from head to tail to preserve their unique shape.

Salads and Dressings

Salads can be served before, during, after or *as* the meal. Nothing refreshes like the clean taste of crisp, cool salad greens, but they can be even tastier when served with your own "house dressing." And once you have made your own crunchy Homemade Seasoned Croutons (p. 93), you'll wonder how you've ever lived without them.

With such a healthy variety of tempting "tossables" to complement them—vegetables, fruits, meat, poultry, fish, eggs—it's no wonder that salads are such a popular part of our diet. But salads don't have to be green. The simple—and simply delicious—versions of old favorites and new flavor compositions in this section will win you high marks, too.

Composed Fruit Salad

When Nature's bounty overwhelms us with luscious, mouth-watering choices, compose a still-life painting of seasonal fruits to please the eye as well as the palate.

For each serving, "compose" a variety of fresh fruits directly on a plate or nestled in a bed of alfalfa sprouts or salad greens. Arrange the fruits, varying the colors and shapes for eye appeal. Slice oranges crosswise into wheels. Make Banana Snowballs, Strawberry Fans and Apple Chevrons (see below). For a delicious and interesting temperature contrast, add a scoop of Strawberry Sorbet (p. 126) (or other fruit flavor) to the arrangement just before serving. At the table, spoon Minty Orange Sauce (opposite) over the fruit.

Banana Snowballs

Peel bananas and cut into 1-inch pieces. Using two forks, dip each piece in a small amount of Minty Orange Sauce, then roll the bananas in shredded coconut. Place on wax paper and refrigerate until serving time. These can be made hours ahead and they won't discolor.

Strawberry Fans

Wash strawberries (do not remove stems) very quickly under running water and dry thoroughly. Do not let them soak in water or they will become soggy. With a sharp knife, cut several slices starting from the tip of the berry almost to the stem but not through it. Gently fan out the slices.

Fig. 1

Fig. 2

Apple Chevrons
Wash and core the apples (Red Delicious). Cut them in half from the stem end through the core and place, cut side down, on a cutting board. Cut each half into 7 even wedges. Dip apples in lemon juice to prevent discoloration. Reassemble apple half and gently push the five middle wedges ½ inch away from the stem end of the apple. Push the three middle slices ½ inch further in the same direction. Then push just the center slice an additional ½ inch in the same direction to form a chevron pattern.

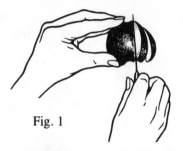
Fig. 1

Fig. 2

Minty Orange Sauce

This is one of the best and most refreshing accompaniments for fruit. It's fantastic as a topping for fruit salad, served over fresh fruit as an appetizer or dessert, or as a dipping sauce.

1	cup sour cream or plain yogurt (or ½ cup of each)
2	tablespoons orange juice concentrate, thawed and undiluted
2	teaspoons confectioner's sugar, or equivalent sugar substitute
1	tablespoon *Mint Oil (see below)*

Combine all ingredients in a mixing bowl. Chill thoroughly to allow the flavors to develop and blend (for several hours if possible). Makes about 1 cup.

Mint Oil

2	cups packed fresh mint leaves
⅓	cup flavorless vegetable oil

In a blender or food processor, puree mint leaves and oil. Store in freezer. Makes ½ cup.

Everyday Hint: For fresh herb flavor all year, make herb oil when herbs are in season. In a blender or food processor, combine 2 cups packed herb leaves and ⅓ cup oil until completely pureed. Freeze in tablespoon-sized portions in ice cube trays or Styrofoam egg cartons. Once frozen, pop the cubes out, store them in a freezer bag and use as needed.

Cucumbers with Sour Cream and Dill

A surprise hint of garlic gives added flavor to this cool and crisp cucumber salad. Use fresh dill when you can find it.

4	**medium cucumbers (about 4 cups sliced)**
1	**tablespoon salt**
1	**cup sour cream**
1	**small clove garlic, minced**
2	**tablespoons chopped fresh dill, or 2 teaspoons dried**

Peel, seed and thinly slice the cucumbers. Place them in a colander, sprinkle them with salt and toss the cucumbers to distribute the salt evenly. Allow the cucumbers to drain for at least 20 minutes to "disgorge" them of excess water. With your hands, squeeze out the remaining water.

In a large bowl, stir together the sour cream, garlic and dill. Stir in the cucumbers. Chill for at least 1 hour to allow the flavors to develop and blend. Makes about 2 cups.

Idea: Cucumbers with Sour Cream and Dill is a wonderful salad or side dish. Try it on your favorite sandwich—it's great with ham or as a sandwich filling all by itself!

 Everyday Hint: If you like cucumbers but they don't like you, it's usually the seeds that are disagreeable. Remove them with an apple corer, or slice them lengthwise and scrape out the seeds with a spoon or your thumb.

 Everyday Hint: Select cucumbers that are small, dark green and firm. Larger, more mature cucumbers have larger seeds and can be bitter. If cucumbers do taste bitter, add a pinch of sugar to sweeten them.

Lemony Mushrooms

The fresh taste of lemon provides a pleasantly sharp companion for these marinated mushrooms. They're especially appealing served in lettuce cups as an appetizer or an antipasto.

1	**pound fresh small mushrooms**
3/4	**cup oil**
1/4	**cup lemon juice**
2	**tablespoons Dijon mustard**
2	**cloves garlic, minced**
1/2	**teaspoon salt**
1/4	**teaspoon pepper**

Clean the mushrooms and cut off part of the stems. Cut large mushrooms in halves or quarters. Place in a bowl or plastic snap-type bag.

In a jar with a lid, shake together the oil, lemon juice, Dijon mustard, garlic, salt and pepper. Pour the marinade over the mushrooms and marinate for 2 hours or overnight. The mushrooms mellow in flavor and moisten slightly as they marinate. Makes about 3 cups.

 Everyday Hint: To clean mushrooms, swish them quickly under running water—don't soak them—and dry them thoroughly. I prefer to use a plastic salad spinner for washing and drying mushrooms. You could use a soft mushroom brush to clean them instead, but it's very time consuming.

 Everyday Hint: Lemons and all citrus fruits yield more juice if they are microwaved on high power for 30 seconds before they are squeezed.

Bibb, Raspberry and Avocado Salad

This exquisite salad is the perfect choice when you want to serve something unique. A beautiful balance of flavors, colors, textures and shapes makes this dish a fashion plate.

2	**small heads Bibb lettuce, or other leafy lettuce**
1	**ripe avocado**
	lemon juice (to prevent avocado from discoloring)
¹/₂	**cup sliced fresh mushrooms**
¹/₂	**cup raspberries, fresh or individually frozen**
	Raspberry Vinaigrette (see below)

Separate, wash and thoroughly dry the lettuce leaves, then arrange them on four salad plates.

Slice the avocado in half lengthwise and twist to separate the halves. With a large serving spoon, scoop out the avocado from the shell, thinly slice it lengthwise and dip the slices in lemon juice. Arrange the avocado slices, mushroom slices and raspberries over the lettuce.

Just before serving, shake the Raspberry Vinaigrette very well and spoon over the salads. Makes 4 servings.

 Everyday Hint: Once cut open, avocados discolor quickly. To prevent this, dip pieces of avocado in lemon juice. Or, save the avocado pit and wrap it with the avocado or place it in any avocado dip before storing in the refrigerator.

 Everyday Hint: Individually frozen raspberries thaw very quickly. Don't defrost before using them in salads or most desserts.

Raspberry Vinaigrette

You don't need expensive raspberry vinegar to make this recipe. Aromatic raspberries perfume this lively vinaigrette and give it a beautiful color.

³/₄	**cup oil**
3	**tablespoons wine vinegar**
1	**tablespoon lemon juice**
¹/₂	**cup raspberries, fresh or individually frozen**
1	**teaspoon sugar**
¹/₂	**teaspoon salt**

Place all the ingredients in a blender or food processor and blend for 1 minute. Strain the vinaigrette through a fine sieve to remove the raspberry seeds. Store in the refrigerator. Shake well before serving. Makes 1 ¹/₄ cups.

Vinaigrette

Vinaigrette salad dressing is the traditional combination of oil and vinegar. It's fun to experiment with different flavored oils or vinegars. Add mustard for a little zip, or your favorite herbs for a specific flavor.

³/₄	**cup oil**
¹/₄	**cup wine vinegar**
	(or part lemon juice)
1	**small clove garlic, finely minced**
¹/₂	**teaspoon Dijon mustard**
¹/₂	**teaspoon salt**
¹/₄	**teaspoon pepper**

Place all the ingredients in a jar with a tight-fitting lid and shake vigorously. Store the vinaigrette in the refrigerator and shake well before serving. Makes 1 cup.

French Dressing

For a spirited French dressing that's simple to make, add 2 tablespoons ketchup and 1 teaspoon paprika to the Vinaigrette recipe above.

Everyday Hint: Pepper has so much more flavor when it is freshly ground. Buy whole peppercorns and a pepper mill and grind your own just before using it on foods or in a recipe.

Marinated Vegetables

The subtleness of this marinade awakens the flavor of the vegetables without overpowering them. The piquantness of lemon juice and Dijon mustard combined with the crunchy vegetables makes a winning combination.

2	**pounds assorted fresh vegetables (see suggestions below)**
1	**cup *Vinaigrette (p. 83)***
2	**tablespoons lemon juice**
1	**tablespoon Dijon mustard**

Clean the vegetables and cut them into bite-sized pieces. For those vegetables that need to be blanched, follow blanching instructions for Crudités (p. 34). Combine the raw and blanched vegetables together. This can be done up to a day ahead and refrigerated.

In a small bowl, mix together the Vinaigrette, lemon juice and mustard. Pour the mixture over the vegetables, toss to coat them evenly and refrigerate for 2 to 4 hours before serving. The vegetables will begin to lose their bright color if stored overnight, but they will still be crisp and flavorful. Makes about 5 cups.

Marinated Vegetables are an excellent substitute for salad and a stimulating way to start a meal. They are good travelers, so take them along for your next picnic.

Suggested vegetables:

Blanched	*Raw*
asparagus	celery
broccoli	cherry tomatoes (whole)
carrots	mushrooms
cauliflower	radishes
green beans	red or green peppers
peas	zucchini or yellow squash

Everyday Hint: When marinating vegetables, meats, etc., place the ingredients in a snap-type plastic bag, squeezing out as much air as possible before sealing it. This allows the marinade to coat the food completely and eliminates the need for stirring or turning.

Caesar Salad

In fine restaurants, this salad is usually prepared with a great flourish at tableside. When you're too hungry to put on a show, this zippy pre-mixed dressing does the trick and tastes great!

1	large head Romaine lettuce
1	cup *Homemade Seasoned Croutons (p. 93)*
4 to 6	anchovies, drained and chopped, optional
1	recipe *Caesar Salad Dressing (see below)*
	extra grated Parmesan cheese

Separate, wash and thoroughly dry the Romaine. Tear the larger leaves into smaller pieces, if desired, and place them in a large bowl with the croutons and anchovies.

Just before serving, shake the Caesar Salad Dressing very well. Pour it over the salad and toss to distribute the dressing evenly. Sprinkle on extra Parmesan cheese. Makes 2 main dish salads or 4 side dish salads.

Caesar Salad Dressing

³/₄	cup oil
¹/₄	cup lemon juice
¹/₄	cup grated Parmesan cheese
2	cloves garlic, finely minced
¹/₂	teaspoon Dijon mustard
¹/₂	teaspoon salt
¹/₄	teaspoon pepper
1	tablespoon anchovy paste or mashed anchovies, optional

Place all the ingredients in a jar with a tight-fitting lid and shake vigorously. Store the dressing in the refrigerator and shake well before serving. Makes about 1 cup.

Spinach Salad with Hot Bacon Dressing

The unexpected addition of golden raisins provides a pleasantly sweet flavor to this popular salad. I like to serve it with Cheesy Herb Bread (p. 33) for a light supper.

8	ounces fresh spinach
4 to 6	strips cooked bacon (reserve drippings for dressing)
¼	cup golden raisins (do not substitute dark raisins)
4	ounces fresh mushrooms, sliced
1	cup *Homemade Seasoned Croutons (p. 93)*
1	recipe *Hot Bacon Dressing (see below)*

Choose small, tender spinach leaves if possible. Tear off the thick stems and veins from the larger leaves. Wash and thoroughly dry the spinach. Tear the leaves into bite-sized pieces and place in a large bowl or individual serving dishes. Crumble the bacon and add it to the spinach along with the raisins, mushrooms and croutons. Just before serving, heat the Hot Bacon Dressing, pour it over the salad and toss to distribute the dressing evenly. Makes 2 main dish salads or 4 side dish salads.

 Everyday Hint: Clean spinach or other curly greens by soaking them in warm water for a few minutes. Immediately rinse the greens in cold water to refresh them. The warm water will slightly soften the leaves to release trapped sand or dirt.

Hot Bacon Dressing

This dressing is the perfect balance of sweet and tangy flavors. When served hot on a salad, it slightly wilts and tenderizes the leaves.

¼	cup bacon drippings
¼	cup red wine vinegar
¼	cup mayonnaise
¼	cup sugar

Heat the bacon drippings and thoroughly stir them together with the vinegar, mayonnaise and sugar. Just before serving, reheat the dressing and pour it over the Spinach Salad. Makes about 1 cup dressing.

 Everyday Hint: When a recipe calls for crumbled bacon or bacon drippings, cut the bacon into small pieces before cooking. Cook the bacon pieces over medium heat, stirring occasionally, so the drippings will not burn before the bacon is crisp.

Homemade Mayonnaise

A staple in most refrigerators, you can make mayonnaise quickly and easily from scratch. It doesn't keep as long as the store-bought kind but has a milder flavor and gives you control over the ingredients.

2	eggs
2	tablespoons vinegar or lemon juice (or 1 tablespoon of each)
1	teaspoon Dijon mustard
1/2	teaspoon salt
1 1/4	cups vegetable oil

In a blender or food processor, place the eggs, vinegar, mustard and salt. Blend for 1 minute or until the eggs double in volume. With the machine running, pour in the oil in a thin, steady stream until the mixture thickens. Store the mayonnaise in the refrigerator. It will become thicker as it chills. Use Homemade Mayonnaise within ten days. Makes 1 1/2 cups.

Herb Mayonnaise

If you like mayonnaise, you'll love Herb Mayonnaise. Add fresh or dried herbs—dill, tarragon, basil, thyme—or a combination of them. Use Herb Mayonnaise just as you would use plain mayonnaise—on sandwiches, mixed in potato or chicken salad, or as a dip for raw vegetables.

1 1/2	cups mayonnaise, store-bought or *Homemade Mayonnaise (see above)*
2	tablespoons minced parsley
1	tablespoon chopped fresh herbs or 1 teaspoon dried
1	small clove garlic

Mix all the ingredients together in a bowl. Refrigerate the Herb Mayonnaise for 1 hour or more to allow the flavors to develop and blend. Makes 1 1/2 cups.

Mayonnaise Salad Dressings

Many popular salad dressings are mayonnaise-based. Create your own and always have a variety of dressings on hand to satisfy everyone's taste. You can make the old standbys or custom design your own exclusive "House Dressing."

Even though the following dressings can be made with plain mayonnaise, I strongly recommend Herb Mayonnaise (p. 87) as the base for them.

Blue Cheese Dressing

Use any blue-veined cheese (Roquefort, Stilton, Gorgonzola) in this distinctive, bold-tasting dressing.

1	cup *Herb Mayonnaise (p. 87)*
1/2	cup sour cream
1/4	cup milk
1/2	cup crumbled blue cheese (4 ounces)

In a bowl, beat together the Herb Mayonnaise, sour cream and milk. Stir in the crumbled blue cheese and chill for several hours to allow the flavors to develop and blend. Makes about 1 1/2 cups.

Russian Dressing

Similar to Thousand Island, you'll relish this lively, authoritative dressing.

1	cup *Herb Mayonnaise (p. 87)*
1/2	cup chili sauce
2	tablespoons milk
1	tablespoon pickle relish

In a bowl, mix together the Herb Mayonnaise, chili sauce, milk and pickle relish. Chill. Makes about 1 1/2 cups.

Creamy Parmesan Cheese Dressing

This full-flavored topping adds gusto to any salad greens.

1	cup *Herb Mayonnaise (p. 87)*
1/2	cup grated Parmesan cheese
1/2	cup milk

In a bowl, mix together the Herb Mayonnaise, Parmesan cheese and milk. Stir until well mixed and chill for several hours to soften the cheese. Stir again before serving. Makes about 1 1/2 cups.

Citrus Mustard Dressing

A more perfect union would be hard to find. This lively dressing has just the right flavor combinations to win everyone's approval.

1	**cup *Herb Mayonnaise* (p. 87)**
¼	**cup spicy brown mustard (do not substitute other mustards)**
¼	**cup grapefruit juice**
1	**tablespoon sugar**

In a bowl, mix together the Herb Mayonnaise, brown mustard, grapefruit juice and sugar. Stir until well mixed. Chill. Makes about 1½ cups.

Lemon Cucumber Dressing

This light and pleasant-tasting dressing is as refreshing and cool as a cucumber.

1	**cup *Herb Mayonnaise* (p. 87)**
1	**cup plain yogurt**
1	**cup finely chopped cucumber**
2	**tablespoons lemon juice**
1	**tablespoon minced onion**

In a bowl, mix together the Herb Mayonnaise, yogurt, cucumber, lemon juice and minced onion. Stir until well mixed, then chill for several hours to allow the flavors to develop and blend. Makes about 2½ cups.

Chicken Almond Salad Veronique

When grapes are used in a recipe, the French call it "Veronique." I call it delicious!

2	pounds chicken breasts (or 3 cups diced cooked chicken)
³/₄	cup *Herb Mayonnaise (p. 87)*
¹/₄	cup sour cream
¹/₂	cup toasted slivered almonds *(p. 46)*
1	cup seedless grapes

Cook the chicken breasts according to the directions for Chicken Pot Pie (p. 52). Save the broth for another purpose. When the chicken breasts are cool enough to handle, remove the skin and bones and cut the breasts into bite-sized pieces.

In a large bowl, stir together the Herb Mayonnaise and sour cream. Add the diced chicken and stir to coat the chicken, then stir in the almonds and grapes. Chill thoroughly before serving.

Serve a scoop of the chicken salad on salad greens or a nest of alfalfa sprouts. Makes 4 servings.

Idea: To make Turkey Almond Salad, substitute diced turkey breast for the chicken. To make Tuna Almond Salad, substitute 2 9¹/₂-oz. cans water-packed, solid white tuna for the chicken.

Idea: Instead of grapes, add sliced fresh mushrooms to the salad.

 Everyday Hint: When dicing chicken or other cooked meats for a salad or casserole, use kitchen scissors instead of a knife. The pieces will be more uniform in size.

Two-step Chicken Pecan Salad

You'll waltz right through this easy version of a tasty everyday favorite. Before adding mayonnaise, the ingredients are tossed with a light oil coating to perk up the flavors. It's a great way to recycle leftover chicken or turkey.

3	**pounds chicken pieces (or 3 cups diced, cooked chicken)**
¹/₂	**cup diced celery**
2	**tablespoons chopped parsley**
1	**teaspoon salt**
¹/₂	**teaspoon pepper**
¹/₂	**teaspoon dried tarragon**
2	**tablespoons oil**
¹/₂	**cup chopped *Toasted Pecans (p. 46)***
¹/₂	**cup mayonnaise**

Cook the chicken according to the directions for the Chicken Pot Pie (p. 52). Save the broth for another purpose. When the chicken is cool enough to handle, remove the skin and bones and cut the chicken into small pieces.

In a large bowl, place the chicken, celery, parsley, salt, pepper, tarragon and oil and stir together until all the ingredients are well mixed. Cover the bowl and refrigerate the chicken for at least 2 hours or overnight. Stir once or twice to blend all the ingredients.

About 1 hour before serving, add the pecans and mayonnaise to the chicken and stir until well coated. Chill before serving. Makes 4 servings.

Marinated Potato Salad

The lightness and blending of subtle flavors make this potato salad a perfect choice for picnics, hot summer days or informal get-togethers with family and friends. I especially like to use small unpeeled red potatoes for their added color and texture.

3	**pounds small red-skinned potatoes or other boiling potatoes**
¹/₂	**cup *Vinaigrette (p. 83)***
¹/₂	**cup sliced green onions**
¹/₄	**cup chopped parsley**
1	**cup *Herb Mayonnaise (p. 87)***

Scrub the potatoes and cut into bite-sized pieces. Boil them in salted water until just tender. Drain the potatoes and set aside to cool slightly.

In a large bowl, stir together the Vinaigrette, green onions and parsley. Toss the warm potatoes with the Vinaigrette mixture and allow them to marinate at room temperature for about 1 hour, stirring occasionally.

Drain off the excess Vinaigrette from the potatoes. Add the mayonnaise and toss it with the potatoes until they are well coated. Cover and refrigerate for at least 2 hours or overnight. Makes about 9 cups.

Hot Potato Salad
Place the potato salad in a baking dish and sprinkle Seasoned Bread Crumbs (p. 20) over the top of the potatoes. For additional flavor and crunch, sprinkle with crisp, crumbled bacon. Bake for 20 to 25 minutes at 350 degrees until the potatoes are hot. This is a great use for leftover potato salad and makes a hearty side dish for dinner.

 Everyday Hint: Make potato salad with "new" potatoes (thin-skinned red or white boiling potatoes) as they hold their shape better than baking potatoes and do not fall apart when stirred. Add dressing to potatoes while they are still warm so they can better absorb the flavors.

Cauliflower Slaw

The full-bodied flavor and crunchy texture make this out-of-the-ordinary slaw a front runner in the list of family favorites.

1	cup *Herb Mayonnaise (p. 87)*
¹/₂	cup sour cream
1	large head cauliflower
1	cup shredded carrot (about 2 medium)
1	cup thinly sliced radishes
2	tablespoons thinly sliced green onion

In a large bowl, mix together the Herb Mayonnaise and sour cream. Cut out the core of the cauliflower and remove the thick stems. Break the florets apart into very small pieces.

Mix the cauliflower, carrots, radishes and green onion together with the dressing. Chill for at least 2 hours or overnight. Makes 5 cups.

Homemade Seasoned Croutons

It's unbelievably easy to make your own seasoned croutons from leftover bread (I prefer French or Italian) or rolls that have been cut into 1-inch cubes. And they taste so much better than the expensive "jaw-breakers" sold in stores. They're terrific served over salads, soups or casseroles.

4	cups bread cubes
¹/₂	cup *Herb Butter (p. 18)*, melted

Preheat oven to 300 degrees.

Place the bread cubes in a large bowl. Pour the melted Herb Butter over the bread cubes and toss to distribute the butter evenly.

Place the bread cubes in a single layer in a baking pan. Bake for 20 to 25 minutes or until lightly browned, stirring every 5 minutes for even toasting.

Allow the croutons to cool completely, then store them in an airtight container. Freeze them for longer storage. Makes 4 cups.

Idea: To make Homemade Parmesan Croutons, add 2 tablespoons Parmesan cheese to the melted Herb Butter before tossing with the bread cubes.

Fabulous Fruit Topping

This recipe has been a favorite in my family for as long as I can remember, and it never fails to get raves. The subtle blend of fruit flavors and whipped cream makes a soft, fluffy dressing that is simply heavenly with fruit. Serve this topping over Composed Fruit Salad (p. 78), any fresh fruits, or use it in making Frozen Fruit Salad (p. 95).

3	**eggs**
½	**cup sugar**
1	**teaspoon cornstarch**
½	**cup pineapple juice**
½	**cup orange juice**
2	**tablespoons lemon juice**
1	**cup heavy cream**

In a saucepan, mix the eggs, sugar, cornstarch, pineapple, orange and lemon juices together. Cook over medium heat, stirring constantly, until the mixture comes to a boil and thickens slightly. Pour it into a bowl, place a piece of plastic wrap directly over the surface of the custard and refrigerate it until completely chilled. (This can be prepared a day ahead.)

In a deep bowl, whip the cream until it forms stiff peaks when the beaters are lifted. Pour the cold custard over the whipped cream and gently fold it in until evenly mixed. Refrigerate until serving time. Makes 4 cups.

 Everyday Hint: Whipping cream beats to its highest volume if the cream, bowl and beaters are cold. Place the bowl and beaters in the freezer before using.

Frozen Fruit Salad

On a hot day you'll especially welcome this luscious combination of refreshing fruits suspended like jewels in a delicately flavored dressing.

1	recipe *Fabulous Fruit Topping (p. 94)*
1	cup berries
1	cup seedless grapes, halved
1	cup orange segments, halved (2 oranges)
1	cup pineapple chunks
1	cup banana slices,
	or 5 cups of any fresh, frozen or canned fruit, well drained

Make Fabulous Fruit Topping. Prepare the fruit, drain it well and place it in a large bowl.

Pour the Fabulous Fruit Topping over the fruit and gently fold it in until all the fruit is coated. Pour the fruit salad into any 2-quart mold, loaf or baking pan. Freeze the mixture for several hours or until it is firm. Allow the salad to thaw slightly before cutting into squares for serving. Makes 10 to 12 servings.

Idea: Freeze individual Frozen Fruit Salads in cupcake paper-lined muffin pans. When frozen, transfer them to an airtight freezer bag to use as needed.

Idea: Freeze the salad in a loaf or baking pan. When frozen, slice or cut it into individual servings, wrap them in plastic wrap and freeze in an airtight freezer bag to use as needed.

Vegetables and Side Dishes

Fresh vegetables have a perfectly wonderful flavor of their own. Since Nature has already shaped them artistically and dressed them in magnificent colors, they rarely need more than a squeeze of lemon or a dab of butter to reach perfection.

But even Mother Nature would applaud these enticing dishes. If you've always shunned soufflés, you're in for a delicious surprise on page 102. These puffy masterpieces are unbelievably simple to make. And don't bypass the terrific Vegetable Terrine (p. 99) and Timbales (p. 98)—they only look and sound fancy.

Vegetable Timbales

Everyone will be captivated by the beauty, smooth texture and delicate flavor of these layered vegetable cups. Mix and match two of your favorite vegetables that are complementary in color and flavor, bake them in custard cups and turn them out to add a decorative touch to any plate.

1	**pound carrots**
2	**tablespoons butter, melted**
2	**tablespoons heavy cream**
2	**eggs**
$1/2$	**teaspoon salt**
$1/4$	**teaspoon pepper**
1	**10-oz. package frozen peas**

Preheat oven to 350 degrees.

Butter 4 $1/2$-cup molds or custard cups and line the bottom of each mold with a circle of buttered wax paper.

Peel and slice the carrots and cook them until tender. Drain, pat dry and puree them in a food processor or blender until smooth. With the food processor running, add 1 tablespoon melted butter, 1 tablespoon cream, 1 egg, $1/4$ teaspoon salt and a pinch of pepper. Fill half of each mold with the pureed carrots.

Cook the peas until tender. Drain and pat dry and puree them in a food processor until smooth. With the food processor running, add the remaining butter, cream, egg, salt and pepper. Spoon the pureed peas over the carrots to fill the mold. Smooth with a knife and cover with circles of buttered wax paper. (The molds can be prepared a day ahead and refrigerated.)

Arrange the molds in a baking pan and place in the oven. Pour boiling water into the pan to reach halfway up the sides of the molds. Bake for 20 minutes. Turn off the oven and with the oven door ajar, let the molds stand in the water for 10 minutes. Remove the molds from the water bath and let them set for 5 minutes. Loosen with a knife and unmold onto a serving plate. (Don't forget to remove the wax paper circles.) Makes 4 servings.

Idea: Make Vegetable Timbales using other vegetables (broccoli, sweet potatoes, cauliflower, spinach, etc.) that are complementary in color and flavor.

Vegetable Terrine

A slice of this elegant vegetable loaf looks stunning on a dinner plate. But it's easily made in a loaf pan with a simple batter and layers of colorful vegetables. Served with Blender Hollandaise Sauce (p. 66), Cheddar Cheese Sauce (p. 107) or just melted butter, it makes a great luncheon dish or light supper.

3	eggs
1	cup milk
$^1/_2$	cup flour
2	teaspoons salt
2	tablespoons butter
2	tablespoons chopped onion
2	10-oz. packages frozen chopped spinach, thawed
1	pound whole carrots
1	pound cauliflower

Preheat oven to 400 degrees.

In a blender or food processor, mix together the eggs, milk, flour and salt.

In a skillet over medium-high heat, heat the butter and cook the onion just until soft. Remove the skillet from the heat. Squeeze all the water out of the spinach. Stir the spinach and one-third of the batter into the skillet and set aside.

Peel the carrots, trim off the ends and partially cook in boiling water for 5 to 7 minutes until they are tender but still crisp. Drain and pat them dry. Separate the cauliflower into florets, slicing the large pieces in half. Partially cook them in boiling water for 3 minutes. Drain and pat dry.

Heavily butter a 2-quart loaf pan and line it with aluminum foil. Butter the foil and layer half the cauliflower to completely cover the bottom of the pan. Pour half of the remaining batter over the cauliflower. Spread half the spinach mixture over the batter. Lay the carrots next to each other lengthwise on top of the spinach. Spread the remaining spinach over the carrots. Top with the remaining cauliflower and press down. Pour the remaining batter over the cauliflower.

Cover the pan with buttered aluminum foil and press down. Place the loaf pan in a larger baking pan and place in the oven. Pour boiling water into the larger pan to reach halfway up the sides of the loaf pan. Bake for 1 hour. Remove the loaf pan from the pan of water and allow it to cool at least 1 hour before unmolding and slicing into 1-inch slices. Makes 6 to 8 side dish servings or 4 main dish servings.

Idea: Vegetable Terrine can be made a day ahead and refrigerated. Slice the loaf into 1-inch slices and place on a baking sheet, cover loosely with buttered wax paper or aluminum foil and heat in a 350 degree oven until hot, about 8 to 10 minutes.

Tomatoes Florentine

In Florence, spinach is used in so many creative ways to make unique and tasty dishes. Here, tomatoes stuffed with Spinach Herb Filling and baked with a Parmesan Bread Crumb topping have a special Florentine touch.

4 to 6	**small tomatoes, or 3 large tomatoes, halved**
1	**teaspoon salt**
1	**recipe *Spinach Herb Filling (p. 67)***
¹/₂	**cup *Parmesan Bread Crumbs (p. 20)***

Preheat oven to 350 degrees.

Cut off the tops of the tomatoes (stem end) and scoop out the seed pockets, leaving the pulp inside. Sprinkle the tomatoes with the salt.

Fill the tomatoes with the Spinach Herb Filling, mounding it slightly, then sprinkle Parmesan Bread Crumbs on top of the filling.

Place the filled tomatoes in ungreased muffin pans for easy handling. Bake for 15 minutes. Remove the tomatoes from the muffin pan with a large spoon. Tomatoes Florentine can be prepared early in the day and baked just before serving. Makes 4 to 6 servings.

 Everyday Hint: Muffin pans are excellent utensils for baking individual foods such as tomatoes, peppers, apples, onions, orange shells, etc. Filling them is much easier and the food is held upright during baking.

Homemade Tomato Sauce

It doesn't have to take hours of stirring and simmering to capture the full flavor of homemade tomato sauce. This easy sauce takes only 30 minutes to make and tastes so much better than store-bought spaghetti sauce.

2	tablespoons oil
1	cup chopped onion
1	clove garlic, minced
1	28-oz. can tomato puree
1	tablespoon chopped parsley
$^1/_2$	teaspoon dried basil
$^1/_2$	teaspoon dried oregano
2	tablespoons grated Parmesan cheese
$^1/_2$	teaspoon salt
$^1/_4$	teaspoon pepper

Heat the oil in a skillet over medium heat. Cook the onion until it is soft but not brown. Stir in the garlic, then add the tomato puree, parsley, basil, oregano, Parmesan cheese, salt and pepper. Stirring occasionally, simmer the sauce for 20 to 30 minutes until it has reduced and thickened. Makes 3 cups.

Idea: To make Homemade Tomato Meat Sauce, in a skillet, lightly brown 1 pound ground meat (beef or beef, pork and veal mixture), drain and stir into the Homemade Tomato Sauce.

Tomato Mousse

This lighter version of robust tomato sauce is a pleasant vegetable alternative. It gives a flavor boost to meat or fish and is a delightfully airy sauce over any pasta.

1	recipe *Homemade Tomato Sauce (see above)*
2	egg whites
$^1/_4$	cup *Parmesan Bread Crumbs (p. 20)*, optional

Make the Homemade Tomato Sauce. In a small bowl, beat the egg whites until they are stiff but not dry. Fold them into the hot sauce.

Gently spoon the mousse into a 1-quart casserole or soufflé dish or into individual serving dishes. Sprinkle Parmesan Bread Crumbs over the top of the mousse.

Serve immediately or keep warm until serving time by placing the casserole or serving dishes in a pan of hot water. Makes 4 to 6 servings.

Spinach Soufflé

If even mentioning the word "soufflé" strikes fear in your heart, you can relax. These recipes are so easy you'll soon be making exquisite soufflés for brunch, lunch or as special side dishes.

1	recipe *Herb White Sauce (p. 107)*, omitting the chicken broth
3	eggs
1	10-oz. package frozen chopped spinach, thawed
$1/2$	cup grated Parmesan cheese
1	teaspoon mustard (Dijon or whole grain)
$1/2$	teaspoon pepper

Preheat oven to 375 degrees.

Butter well a straight-sided 5- or 6-cup baking or soufflé dish. Set aside.

Make the Herb White Sauce. Since the liquid has been cut in half, this sauce will be very thick.

Separate the egg yolks from the whites. Beat the egg yolks into the sauce (see Everyday Hint on opposite page).

Squeeze the water out of the spinach.

In a large bowl, stir together the spinach, Parmesan cheese, mustard and pepper. Stir in the sauce and mix well.

In a separate bowl, beat the egg whites with an electric mixer until they are foamy, then add a pinch of salt (this helps the whites hold their shape). Continue to beat until the whites stand up in stiff peaks when the beaters are lifted. Rapidly stir one-quarter of the egg whites into the spinach mixture to lighten it, then gently fold in the remaining egg whites. Spoon the mixture into the buttered soufflé dish. Smooth out the top of the soufflé and place it on the bottom rack of the oven. Bake for 25 to 30 minutes until lightly browned on top and until a cake tester or skewer inserted sideways into the center of the puffed soufflé comes out clean. (Don't insert the tester down into the center as for a cake, or the soufflé will deflate.) The soufflé should be moist and creamy inside. Serve immediately. Makes 4 servings.

Note: A soufflé can be assembled at least 1 hour before baking. Just place a large pot or bowl upside down over the soufflé to keep out drafts. Or, if you prefer, you can prepare all the ingredients hours ahead except for the egg whites, which should be beaten just before adding them to the rest of the soufflé mixture. A baked soufflé doesn't like to wait for anyone, but if it must, turn the oven off with the oven door ajar and it will wait for an extra 5 minutes.

Cheese Soufflé

1	recipe *Herb White Sauce (p. 107)*, omitting the chicken broth
1	cup grated cheddar cheese (4 ounces)
1	teaspoon mustard (Dijon or whole grain)
½	cup grated Parmesan cheese
3	eggs

Preheat oven to 375 degrees.

Butter well a straight-sided 5- or 6-cup baking or soufflé dish. Set aside.

Make the Herb White Sauce. Stir in the cheddar cheese, mustard and Parmesan cheese. Stir until the cheddar cheese melts.

Separate the egg yolks from the whites. Beat the yolks into the cheese mixture (see Everyday Hint below). Beat the egg whites and follow the same procedures as for the Spinach Soufflé recipe. Makes 4 servings.

Idea: To make asparagus, cauliflower or broccoli soufflé, cook a 10-oz. package of the frozen vegetable (or 1 pound fresh). Drain well, mash and substitute the vegetable for the spinach in the Spinach Soufflé recipe.

 Everyday Hint: Separate egg yolks from whites when eggs are cold. Egg whites beaten after they have come to room temperature will whip faster and have greater volume.

 Everyday Hint: When adding egg yolks to a hot liquid, stir a small amount of hot liquid into the egg yolks to warm them gradually before adding them to the rest of the hot liquid.

 Everyday Hint: When making a soufflé, don't open the oven door while it's baking and don't set the finished soufflé directly on a cold surface or it may deflate.

Potato Wedgies

Here's an easy and fun way to serve baked potatoes—they're especially good when stuffed. For a tasty and nutritious snack serve them with your favorite dip.

4	**baking potatoes**
3	**tablespoons butter, or** *Herb Butter (p. 18)*, **melted**
	garlic salt or seasoned salt

Preheat oven to 425 degrees.

Scrub potatoes and quarter them lengthwise. If potatoes are very large, cut into sixths. Place the wedgies, skin side down, in a baking pan. Brush them with melted butter and sprinkle with garlic salt or seasoned salt.

Bake for about 45 minutes. Test with a fork for doneness. Serve with sour cream and chives, if you wish. Makes 4 to 6 servings.

Stuffed Potato Wedgies

When the potatoes are cool enough to handle, make a slit lengthwise in each wedgie. Fill the slit with shredded cheese (cheddar, jack, Parmesan). Sprinkle with crumbled bacon, cooked sausage, ground beef or chopped ham. Reheat the potato wedgies at 475 degrees for 5 to 10 minutes until the cheese melts and the skin is crisp. You can bake the potato wedgies hours in advance, then fill and reheat just before serving.

 Everyday Hint: It's important to bake potatoes in a *hot* oven for the inside to be fluffy and the outside to be crisp.

Potatoes Parmesan

The wonderful flavor and aroma of fragrant herbs make this simple dish one that you'll choose to serve often.

4	**cups baking potatoes (about 2 pounds)**
1	**cup** *Parmesan Bread Crumbs (p. 20)*
½	**cup** *Herb Butter (p. 18)*

Preheat oven to 425 degrees.

Wash and slice the potatoes, peeled or unpeeled, ⅛ inch thick. Pat the slices dry with paper towels. Sprinkle ¼ cup bread crumbs into a buttered 9-inch baking pan. Top the crumbs with one-third of the potatoes, then dot with one-third of the butter. Repeat the layers with the remaining crumbs, potatoes and butter, ending with crumbs.

Bake for 45 minutes to 1 hour until the potatoes are cooked and starting to crisp around the edges. Makes 4 to 6 servings.

Cheesy Potatoes au Gratin

Cheddar Cheese Sauce makes this hearty, bubbly mixture the smoothest and best scalloped potato dish you've ever tasted.

4   **cups baking potatoes (about 2 pounds)**
1   **recipe** *Cheddar Cheese Sauce (p. 107)*

Preheat oven to 350 degrees.

Scrub the potatoes and slice them, peeled or unpeeled, 1/8 inch thick. Layer the potatoes in a well-buttered 9 by 13-inch baking dish and pour the Cheddar Cheese Sauce over the potatoes.

Bake for 1 hour and 15 minutes until the potatoes are tender. Makes 4 to 6 servings.

Brussels Sprouts Parmesan

Cook strong-flavored vegetables in chicken broth to mellow their flavor. A sprinkling of Parmesan cheese provides a fitting accent to these Brussels sprouts.

1   **10-oz. package frozen Brussels sprouts, or 1 pound fresh**
1/2   **cup chicken broth**
2   **tablespoons butter, softened**
2   **tablespoons grated Parmesan cheese**

Cook the Brussels sprouts in the chicken broth until tender. Drain them well. Toss the sprouts in the butter, then sprinkle them with Parmesan cheese. Makes 4 servings.

Vegetables in Alfredo Sauce

Perk up everyday vegetables—either fresh or frozen—with the easy addition of Alfredo Sauce.

1   **10-oz. package frozen or 1 pound fresh vegetables (cauliflower, broccoli, green beans or any vegetable mixture)**
1/4   **cup** *Alfredo Sauce (p. 23),* **room temperature**

Cook the vegetables until tender and drain them well. Toss the hot vegetables with the Alfredo Sauce and serve immediately. Makes 4 servings.

Carrots in Caramel Sauce

Vegetables served in a sweet sauce with a hint of cinnamon are a Southern tradition. But no matter where you live, your family will love carrots basted with this rich caramel sauce.

1½	**pounds carrots (or sweet potatoes)**
¼	**cup butter (½ stick)**
¼	**cup sugar**
¼	**cup heavy cream**
½	**teaspoon cinnamon**

Peel the carrots, cut them into large chunks and cook them until tender. Drain the carrots very well and set aside.

Melt the butter in a saucepan over high heat. Add the sugar and stir rapidly for 1 minute until the mixture just turns golden brown. The color changes very quickly so don't let the sugar burn.

Pour in the cream and cinnamon and stir vigorously for 2 minutes until the mixture thickens and looks like caramel. Add the carrots and stir to coat. Makes 4 to 6 servings.

Sweet Potatoes à l'Orange

Whipped sweet potatoes are a delicious change from everyday mashed potatoes. Here, the zesty orange flavor enhances the sweetness of the potatoes. Serve them in hollowed-out orange shells for an extra-special presentation.

2	**pounds sweet potatoes, cooked and peeled**
¼	**cup butter (½ stick), softened**
¼	**cup sour cream**
2	**eggs**
2	**tablespoons brown sugar**
1	**teaspoon grated orange peel**
¼	**cup orange juice**
½	**cup chopped *Toasted Pecans (p. 46)***

Preheat oven to 350 degrees.

In a mixer or food processor whip the sweet potatoes. Beat in the butter, sour cream, eggs, brown sugar, orange peel and orange juice.

Place the sweet potatoes in a buttered 1½-quart casserole and top with the pecans. (This can be made ahead to this point.) Bake for 20 minutes or until heated through. Makes 6 servings.

Idea: Spoon the potato mixture into a pastry bag with a large decorative tip. Squeeze the mixture into 6 hollowed-out orange shells. Sprinkle with chopped pecans and refrigerate. Heat the potatoes in the orange shells for 5 to 10 minutes before serving.

Herb White Sauce

Basic white sauce becomes much more appealing to the taste buds with the special addition of Herb Butter. Use it in creamed dishes, casseroles or over vegetables.

¹/₄	cup *Herb Butter (p. 18)*, softened
¹/₄	cup flour
1	cup chicken broth
1	cup milk

Beat the softened Herb Butter and flour together to form a paste.

Heat the broth and the milk in a saucepan over high heat until boiling. Rapidly stir the butter and flour paste into the boiling liquid until it has thickened.

Lower the heat to medium and continue stirring for 2 to 3 minutes to cook the flour. Makes 2 cups.

Cheddar Cheese Sauce

The distinctive sharpness of cheddar makes this cheese sauce ideal with ham, vegetables or in casseroles.

1	recipe *Herb White Sauce (see above)*
1	cup grated cheddar cheese (4 ounces)
¹/₂	teaspoon mustard (Dijon or whole grain)

Make the Herb White Sauce. When the sauce has thickened, add the cheese and mustard and stir until the cheese has melted. Makes 2¹/₃ cups.

Biscuits, Muffins and More

Quick breads are quick to make because there's no waiting for them to rise as you must do for yeast breads. This section is full of delicious quick breads and flavorful butters and spreads. There are sweet and fruit-filled choices for breakfast as well as savory selections to brighten up dinner.

If you've never made breads before, here's your chance. I've simplified all of these recipes so that you can make any of them with complete confidence. But I must caution you: close all the doors and windows while any of these breads are baking, or else the heavenly aroma will have the whole neighborhood flocking to your door.

Basic Biscuit Mix

This is the same Basic Biscuit Mix as in the Everyday Basics chapter. For your convenience and easy reference it is given again here.

2	cups flour
1	tablespoon baking powder
$^1/_2$	teaspoon salt
$^1/_2$	cup butter (1 stick), cold

In a large bowl thoroughly mix the flour, baking powder and salt. Using a food processor, pastry blender or 2 knives, cut in the butter until it is the size of very small peas and distributed throughout the dry ingredients.

Store Basic Biscuit Mix in plastic bags and refrigerate or freeze until you are ready to use it.

Homemade Biscuits

They're what memories are made of, yet biscuits are so quick and simple to make. They can also be prepared a day ahead, refrigerated on a baking sheet, then baked just before serving. The secret to making tender biscuits is a gentle touch. Do not over-knead the dough and do not add any more flour than necessary.

1	recipe *Basic Biscuit Mix (see above)*
$^3/_4$	cup milk

Preheat oven to 425 degrees.

To mix: Place the Basic Biscuit Mix in a large bowl. Pour in the milk and stir with a fork just until the dry ingredients are moistened and the dough begins to chase itself around the bowl. Do not overmix! Turn the dough out onto a lightly floured surface and press together.

To knead: Fold the top half of the dough toward you. Using the palms of your hands, gently push the dough away from you, then turn the dough a quarter turn. Repeat the fold, push, turn procedure 8 to 10 times or just until the dough holds together. If the dough seems too sticky, add a little more flour.

To shape: With a rolling pin, gently roll the dough from the center out until the dough is $^1/_2$ inch thick. With a floured 2 to 3-inch round cutter, cut the circles as closely together as possible. Place them 2 inches apart on an ungreased baking sheet. Press together (do not knead) the remaining scraps of dough and cut more biscuits. Or to save time and re-rolling, cut the biscuit dough into 2 to 3-inch squares instead of circles.

To bake: Bake for 12 to 15 minutes in a preheated 425 degree oven until the biscuits are lightly brown. Makes about 12 biscuits.

Homemade Drop Biscuits
In a large bowl, place 1 recipe Basic Biscuit Mix and 1 cup milk. Follow the mixing instructions for Homemade Biscuits (see opposite) except instead of kneading, drop spoonfuls of biscuit dough 2 inches apart onto an ungreased baking sheet.

Idea: Spoon drop biscuits over casseroles, stews or Fruit Cobbler (p. 140).

Buttermilk Biscuits
In a large bowl, stir together 1 recipe Basic Biscuit Mix and ½ teaspoon baking soda. Pour in 1 cup buttermilk and stir with a fork just until the dry ingredients are moistened and the dough begins to chase itself around the bowl. Do not overmix! Follow the kneading, shaping and baking instructions for Homemade Biscuits (see opposite).

Buttermilk Biscuits go well with Beef Burgundy (p. 62) or any hearty dish.

Cheese Biscuits
Follow the recipe for Homemade Biscuits (see opposite) except add 1 cup grated cheddar cheese to the Basic Biscuit Mix. Cheese Biscuits and a crisp, green salad make a perfect light lunch.

Herb Biscuits
Follow the recipe for Homemade Biscuits (see opposite) or Buttermilk Biscuits (see above) but do not bake. Spread the top of each unbaked biscuit with 2 teaspoons of softened Herb Butter (p. 18). In a round cake or pie pan, arrange the biscuits in a circle, buttered side up, overlapping the biscuits slightly.

Bake for 15 to 20 minutes until the biscuits are golden brown. Herb Biscuits are especially inviting when served with meats.

Idea: If you use refrigerator biscuits instead of homemade biscuits, adjust the baking time according to package instructions.

Biscuit Tea Ring

Shaped like a festive wreath, this easy tea ring is a treat for weekends and holidays and will bring you lots of compliments.

Rich Biscuit Dough:

1	recipe *Basic Biscuit Mix (p. 110)*
2	tablespoons sugar
1	egg
¹/₂	cup milk

Filling:

1	tablespoon butter, melted
¹/₄	cup sugar
¹/₂	teaspoon cinnamon
¹/₄	cup chopped pecans

Glaze:

1	tablespoon butter, softened
1	cup confectioner's sugar, sifted
¹/₂	teaspoon vanilla
¹/₄	teaspoon almond extract
4	teaspoons milk
	red and green candied cherries, optional

Preheat oven to 400 degrees.

In a bowl, combine the Basic Biscuit Mix and sugar. In a measuring cup, slightly beat the egg, then pour in enough milk to measure ³/₄ cup. Pour into the dry ingredients and stir with a fork just until the dry ingredients are moistened and the dough begins to chase itself around the bowl. Do not overmix!

Follow the kneading instructions for Homemade Biscuits (p. 110), except on a floured surface roll the dough into a 9 by 16-inch rectangle about ¹/₄ inch thick. Spread melted butter over the surface of the dough. Combine the sugar and cinnamon, then sprinkle evenly over the butter. Top with chopped pecans. (See illustration opposite.)

Starting with a long side of the rectangle, roll the dough like a jelly roll. Transfer the dough to a cookie sheet and form into a circle. Using scissors or a sharp knife, cut three-quarters of the way from the outside toward the center to make 12 individual rolls still attached in the center. Do not cut through the center of the ring. Turn each roll on its side so the swirl is facing upward. Bake for 20 to 25 minutes or until golden brown.

To prepare the glaze, beat the softened butter with the confectioner's sugar in a small bowl. Beat in the vanilla, almond extract and milk. Drizzle the glaze over the warm rolls. Cut red cherries in half and green cherries into quarters for "leaves." Arrange over the glazed tea ring. Makes 10 to 12 servings.

Savory Biscuit Pinwheels

Sausage and biscuits taste great together, so why not make them together to start with? These savory pinwheels have the added bite of cheddar cheese and make a terrific breakfast treat.

1	recipe *Basic Biscuit Mix (p. 110)*
³/₄	cup milk
1	tablespoon butter, melted
1	cup cooked crumbled sausage or chopped ham
1	cup grated cheddar cheese

Preheat oven to 400 degrees.

In a bowl, combine the Basic Biscuit Mix and milk. Stir with a fork just until the dry ingredients are moistened and the dough begins to chase itself around the bowl. Do not overmix!

Follow the kneading instructions for Homemade Biscuits (p. 110), except on a floured surface roll the dough into a 9 by 16-inch rectangle about ¼ inch thick. Spread the melted butter over the surface of the dough. Sprinkle the sausage or ham evenly over the dough, then sprinkle the cheese over the meat.

Starting with a long side of the rectangle, roll the dough like a jelly roll. Using a knife, cut the roll into 10 to 12 slices. Lay the slices, pinwheel side up, on a lightly greased baking sheet.

Bake for 15 to 20 minutes until golden brown. Makes 10 to 12 pinwheels.

Idea: Make pinwheel muffins by placing the unbaked slices, pinwheel side up, in well-greased muffin pans.

Biscuit Tea Ring

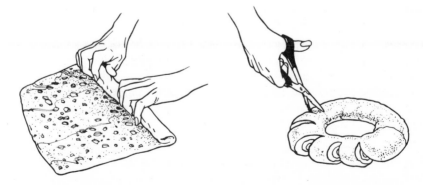

Fig. 1   Fig. 2

Biscuit Sweet Rolls

This tempting but time-saving recipe lets you have your favorite sweet roll flavors anytime.

1   recipe *Basic Biscuit Mix (p. 110)*
1   **cup milk**
¹/₄   **cup fruit preserves, pie or pastry filling,
        or *Streusel Topping (p. 117)***
Glaze:
1   **cup confectioner's sugar, sifted**
1   **tablespoon milk**
¹/₂   **teaspoon vanilla**

Preheat oven to 425 degrees.

Place the Basic Biscuit Mix in a large bowl. Pour in the milk and stir with a fork until the dry ingredients are just moistened. Do not overmix! With a tablespoon, drop 10 to 12 biscuits 2 inches apart on an ungreased baking sheet. With the back of a teaspoon, spread the dough into a smooth circle and make an indentation in the center of each biscuit. Fill the center with a teaspoonful of preserves, filling or streusel. Bake for 12 to 15 minutes or until lightly brown.

To prepare the glaze, mix together the sugar, milk and vanilla in a small bowl. Drizzle the glaze over warm sweet rolls. Serve warm. Makes about 10 to 12 sweet rolls.

Quick Biscuit Donuts

Using an electric fry pan, you can make these donuts on the spot for camping trips, bake sales and church bazaars. They'll disappear as quickly as you can make them.

1   **can refrigerator biscuits
        oil for frying
        choice of topping**

Separate the biscuits and lightly flour them. Punch out a small circle from the center of each biscuit to form the donut hole.

In a heavy skillet or electric fry pan, heat 1 to 2 inches of oil to 375 degrees. Carefully slide the donuts into the oil and fry for just a minute on one side until golden brown. Carefully flip the donuts and brown the other side for another 30 seconds. With a slotted spoon or fork, remove the donuts and drain them on paper towels. Fry donuts right before serving and eat them warm. Don't forget to fry the donut holes!

Roll warm donuts in cinnamon sugar or confectioner's sugar, or, easier yet, shake the sugar and donuts in a plastic or paper bag. If you prefer, glaze or ice the donut tops and sprinkle with nuts, coconut or chocolate sprinkles. Serve warm. Makes 8 to 10 donuts.

Muffins

Mmmmmm muffins! Such a heart-warming way to greet the day. They're equally satisfying for lunch or tea time—you can even make savory ones for dinner.

2	**cups flour**
1/4	**cup sugar**
1	**tablespoon baking powder**
1/2	**teaspoon salt**
1	**egg**
1	**cup milk**
1/4	**cup butter (1/2 stick), melted**

Preheat oven to 400 degrees.

In a large bowl, thoroughly mix the flour, sugar, baking powder and salt. In another bowl, stir the egg, milk and butter until they are well blended. Pour the liquid ingredients over the dry mixture and stir with a fork until the dry ingredients are just moistened. Do not overmix! Pour the batter into greased muffin pans.

Bake for 20 to 25 minutes until the muffins are golden brown. Makes 12 muffins.

Jelly-filled Muffins
Follow the recipe for Muffins (see above), except before baking, drop a teaspoonful of jelly or preserves on the top of each muffin. With the back of a spoon, press the jelly into the center of the muffin. Top with Streusel Topping (p. 117) if desired.

Blueberry Muffins
Follow the directions for Muffins (see above), except stir an additional 2 tablespoons sugar and 1/2 teaspoon nutmeg (optional) into the dry ingredients. Stir in the liquid ingredients until the dry ingredients are just moistened, then gently fold in 1 cup blueberries, fresh or individually frozen (unthawed).

Cheddar Cheese Muffins
Follow the directions for Muffins (see above), except stir 1 to 1 1/2 cups grated cheddar cheese into the dry ingredients before adding the liquid ingredients. The added sharpness of the muffins makes them a perfect complement to a crispy green salad.

Herb Cheese Muffins
Follow the directions for Muffins (see above), except beat 1/2 cup or 4 ounces softened Herb Cheese (p. 24) and 1 teaspoon dill or other dried herb into the liquid ingredients until well blended, before stirring into the dry ingredients.

Sour Cream Muffins

Sour cream is a plus in many recipes, but it is especially flattering to quick breads.

2	**cups flour**
1/4	**cup sugar**
1	**tablespoon baking powder**
1/2	**teaspoon baking soda**
1/2	**teaspoon salt**
2	**eggs**
1	**cup sour cream**
1/4	**cup butter (1/2 stick), melted**

Preheat oven to 400 degrees.

In a large bowl, thoroughly mix the flour, sugar, baking powder, baking soda and salt. In another bowl, stir the eggs, sour cream and butter until well blended. Pour the liquid ingredients over the dry mixture and stir with a fork until the dry ingredients are just moistened. Do not overmix! Pour the batter into greased muffin pans.

Bake for 20 to 25 minutes until the muffins are golden brown. Makes 12 muffins.

Sour Cream Coffee Cake

The rich, crunchy topping provides a fitting contrast to the delicate flavor of this finely textured coffee cake.

Preheat oven to 400 degrees.

Follow the recipe for Sour Cream Muffins (see above), except spread muffin batter into a greased 8- or 9-inch cake pan. Sprinkle on Streusel Topping (p. 117).

Bake for 25 to 30 minutes until a toothpick or cake tester inserted in the center of the cake comes out clean. Makes 10 to 12 servings.

Sour Cream Corn Muffins

Try these for a pleasant change of pace from good old cornbread.

1	**recipe *Sour Cream Muffins (see above)***
1	**8-oz. can cream-style corn**

Preheat oven to 400 degrees.

Follow the directions for Sour Cream Muffins, except stir cream-style corn into the liquid ingredients before combining with the dry ingredients.

Bake for 20 to 25 minutes until the muffins are golden brown. Makes 12 muffins.

Apple Streusel Muffins

These muffins will remind you of the heavenly goodness of apple crumb pie.

1	recipe *Sour Cream Muffins (see opposite)*
1	teaspoon cinnamon
2	cups diced tart apples (Granny Smith), or 1 cup chunky applesauce
1	recipe *Streusel Topping (see below)*

Preheat oven to 400 degrees.

Follow the directions for Sour Cream Muffins, except stir cinnamon into the dry ingredients and stir diced apples or applesauce into the liquid ingredients before mixing. Sprinkle the streusel mixture over the tops of the muffins before baking.

Bake for 20 to 25 minutes until the muffins are golden brown. Makes 12 muffins.

Streusel Topping

¼	cup flour
¼	cup sugar (white or brown)
1	teaspoon cinnamon
2	tablespoons butter, softened
½	cup finely chopped nuts

In a small bowl, stir together the flour, sugar and cinnamon. With a fork or your fingers, thoroughly blend in the butter, then stir in the nuts. Sprinkle over muffins, coffee cake or biscuit sweet rolls before baking. For variety, add a sprinkling of other favorite spices such as nutmeg, cardamom, ginger, cloves or mace.

Bran Muffins

These healthy and hearty muffins are good for you and good-tasting, too.

2	eggs
1	cup buttermilk
1/4	cup oil
2	cups bran cereal (not flakes), or raw (miller's) bran
1	cup flour
1/4	cup sugar
1	tablespoon baking powder
1/2	teaspoon baking soda
1/2	teaspoon salt
1	teaspoon cinnamon
1	cup raisins, optional

Preheat oven to 400 degrees. In a large bowl, stir together the eggs, buttermilk and oil until well blended. Stir in the bran and set aside to soak for 5 minutes. In another bowl, thoroughly mix the flour, sugar, baking powder, baking soda, salt and cinnamon. Stir in the raisins. Pour the bran mixture over the dry ingredients and stir until the dry ingredients are just moistened. Pour the batter into greased muffin pans. If you use raw bran instead of bran cereal, the muffins will not be as sweet, so add more sugar if you wish. Bake for 20 to 25 minutes. Makes 12 muffins.

Banana Bran Muffins

This is my favorite bran muffin. It's wonderful with Strawberry Butter (p. 120).

2	cups raw (miller's) bran
1	cup flour
1/2	cup raw wheat germ
1/2	cup brown sugar
1	tablespoon baking powder
1/2	teaspoon baking soda
2	teaspoons cinnamon
2	eggs
1	cup buttermilk
1/4	cup butter, melted
1	cup mashed ripe bananas (about 2 medium bananas)
1	cup chopped nuts, optional

Preheat oven to 400 degrees. In a large bowl, thoroughly mix the bran, flour, wheat germ, brown sugar, baking powder, baking soda and cinnamon. In another bowl, stir together the eggs, buttermilk, melted butter and bananas until well blended. Pour the liquid ingredients over the dry ingredients and stir until the dry ingredients are just moistened. Stir in the nuts. Pour the batter into greased muffin pans. Bake for 20 to 25 minutes. Makes 12 muffins.

Stuffin' Muffins

These aren't real muffins, they just look like muffins! They're a terrific accompaniment for poultry or pork. Make extras to freeze and have on hand.

Scoop any stuffing mixture into well-buttered muffin pans. (Use either the regular or mini-muffin size.) Pat the stuffing down to form the shape of a muffin. Bake at 325 to 375 degrees (the exact oven temperature is not important) for about 20 minutes until nicely browned (Mini Stuffin' Muffins take less time). Adjust the baking time to your personal preference in crispness.

Apricot Cornbread Stuffing

An ideal combination—Mini Stuffin' Muffins served with Cornish Hens with Savory Apricot Sauce (p. 57).

8	cups cornbread (12-oz. package cornbread muffin mix)
1	cup dried apricots (6 ounces), finely sliced
3/4	cup water
1	egg
1/2	cup butter (1 stick)
1/2	cup chopped celery
1/2	cup chopped onion
2	tablespoons chopped parsley
1/4	teaspoon pepper
1	cup chopped pecans

Preheat oven to 400 degrees.

Make the cornbread according to package directions except thinly spread the batter in a well-greased 12 by 15-inch baking pan. Bake for 10 to 15 minutes until golden brown. Cool, cut cornbread into 1-inch squares and place in a large bowl.

Soak the apricots in the 3/4 cup water for 10 minutes. Lightly beat the egg and stir into the apricots. In a skillet, heat the butter. Stir in the celery, onion, parsley and pepper. Cook over medium-low heat until softened but not browned, then stir into the cornbread. Add the apricot mixture and pecans to the stuffing and mix thoroughly.

Use Apricot Cornbread Stuffing to stuff poultry or pork, or to make Stuffin' Muffins (see above). Makes 12 muffins or 30 mini muffins.

Fruit Butters

Berries show off their naturally beautiful colors, and breads never tasted better. Serve Fruit Butters with biscuits, muffins, nutbreads, waffles, pancakes or toast. Make a variety of butters and freeze them in small or individual portions. Keep them on hand for thoughtful gifts, unexpected company and a yummy for your family's tummy.

Strawberry Butter

It's sheer perfection on Homemade Biscuits (p. 110).

1	cup butter (2 sticks), softened
2	teaspoons lemon juice
¹/₂	cup confectioner's sugar
1	cup strawberries, fresh or frozen, thawed (or blueberries, raspberries, peaches, etc.)

Using a food processor or mixer, beat the butter until it is light and fluffy. Beat in the lemon juice and confectioner's sugar. (Depending on the sweetness of the fruit, use more or less sugar.) Mash the fruit and beat it into the butter a spoonful at a time until well blended. It is important to add the berries slowly so they can be absorbed evenly. Makes about 2 cups.

Mound the butter into small serving bowls and serve with any bread.

Blueberry Butter: It's the crowning touch for Blueberry Muffins (p. 115).

Raspberry Butter: This makes a special event out of toast.

Peach Butter: The delicate flavor enhances any muffin. If the peaches are pale, add a strawberry or two to make them blush.

 Everyday Hint: Fruit Butters freeze beautifully. Clear plastic disposable glasses make attractive serving and freezing containers and allow the beauty of the fruit to show through.

Cinnamon Honey Butter

Everyone will be buzzing around the breakfast table when you serve this yummy spread on toast, waffles, breads or pancakes.

1	cup butter (2 sticks), softened
1	teaspoon cinnamon
¹/₄	cup honey

In a small bowl, beat the butter until fluffy. Add the cinnamon and slowly beat in the honey. Makes 1¹/₄ cups.

 Everyday Hint: When measuring honey, corn syrup or molasses, coat or spray the inside of the measuring cup with oil. The honey will pour right out for a more accurate measure.

Cream Cheese Spreads

Nothing could be easier to whip up than these flavorful combinations—yet they're the crowning touch for biscuits and muffins and make a winning spread for nutbreads.

Orange Cream Cheese Spread

1	**3-oz. package cream cheese, softened**
3	**tablespoons orange marmalade**

In a small bowl, beat the cream cheese until it is smooth and fluffy. Beat in the marmalade, then refrigerate for several hours to allow the flavor to develop. Makes about 1/2 cup.

Pineapple Cherry Cream Cheese Spread

1	**3-oz. package cream cheese, softened**
2	**tablespoons chopped maraschino cherries**
2	**tablespoons crushed pineapple**
2	**tablespoons finely chopped pecans**

In a small bowl, beat the cream cheese until it is smooth and fluffy. Beat in the cherries, pineapple and pecans. Refrigerate for several hours to allow the flavors to develop and blend. Makes about 1/2 cup.

Date Walnut Cream Cheese Spread

1	**3-oz. package cream cheese, softened**
2	**tablespoons chopped dates**
2	**tablespoons chopped walnuts**

In a small bowl, beat the cream cheese until it is smooth and fluffy. Beat in the dates and walnuts. Refrigerate for several hours to allow the flavor to develop. Makes about 1/2 cup.

Desserts

My favorite food is dessert. Any kind of dessert will do, but if it's chocolate, that's even better. For dinner parties I plan the meal around the dessert. In restaurants I read the dessert selection first to see how much room I have to leave. There, I've confessed it. Now I feel better.

The hardest part of writing this book was narrowing down the number of desserts to be included. I've tried to provide a variety of flavors and types of desserts that would appeal to every taste, any occasion and all ages. Some are more elaborate and look difficult, but they're all very easy to make.

Fellow chocolate lovers won't want to miss "60-Second" Chocolate Mousse (p. 124), the easy-to-make Chocolate Truffles (p. 142) or the accurately named Sinfully Rich Chocolate Torte (p. 132). But you'll also find light and elegant Frozen Strawberry Mousse (p. 126) and Poached Pears (p. 136). Be sure not to miss the Butter Pecan Ice Cream (p. 129). You can make it without an ice cream maker and it's so good I should have given it a foreign name.

"60 Second" Chocolate Mousse

The classic French version of this heavenly dessert takes forever to make and you still have a big mess to clean up. This one takes only 60 seconds and you can't tell the difference!

1	cup semi-sweet chocolate chips or pieces (6 ounces)
1	egg
1	teaspoon vanilla, or 1 tablespoon liqueur (Grand Marnier, Cognac, Amaretto, Kahlua, etc.)
1	cup heavy cream

Place the chocolate, egg and flavoring in a blender or food processor. In a saucepan or microwave oven, scald the cream until little bubbles form around the edges, but do not boil it. With the machine running, pour in the hot cream and blend for 1 minute until the chocolate is melted and smooth.

Pour the chocolate mousse into 4 individual serving glasses or bowls. Cool slightly, then cover with plastic wrap. Refrigerate the mousse for several hours until set. If you prefer, the mousse can be made ahead and stored in the freezer for later use.

Before serving, top with whipped cream and shaved chocolate or Chocolate Leaves (see opposite) if desired. Makes 4 servings.

Idea: This makes a very thick mousse. If you prefer to lighten it a little, beat 2 egg whites until stiff but not dry and fold into the mousse before refrigerating. This also increases the number of servings.

Charlotte Mousse

This simplified version of the classic ladyfinger-lined, molded mousse (pictured on the back cover) is showy, yet simple to make with store-bought cookies.

2	recipes *"60 Second" Chocolate Mousse (see above)* Ladyfingers, Milano or Pirouette cookies, or other thin, narrow butter cookies (enough to encircle the mousse)

Make a double recipe of Chocolate Mousse and set aside.

If the cookies are "sandwiched" together, separate them and set aside. Line a straight-sided, flat-bottomed 1-quart bowl or soufflé dish with a double layer of plastic wrap, leaving several inches extending over the top of the bowl for easier unmolding.

Pour the mousse into the bowl and place it in the freezer until firm. Up to an hour before serving, remove the mousse from the freezer and lift it out of the mold using the plastic wrap as a handle. Invert the mousse onto a serving dish and remove the plastic.

Stand the cookies, touching each other, around the sides of the mousse. Gently press the cookies into the mousse. Garnish with whipped cream and Chocolate Leaves (below) if desired. Refrigerate until serving time. Makes 8 to 10 servings.

 Everyday Hint: To split Milano-type chocolate-filled cookies, place them on a baking sheet in a 300 degree oven for about 5 minutes to slightly soften the chocolate. Slide the cookies apart and let cool.

Chocolate Leaves

Chocolate leaves are very impressive, so don't tell anyone how easy *they are to make. Use them to dress up any dessert—even a Twinkie can go formal!*

Use any firm, non-poisonous leaf that has good vein structure on the underside, such as rose, ficus, magnolia, lemon. Leave a small stem on the leaf for easier handling. Rinse the leaves and dry thoroughly.

Melt several ounces of semi-sweet chocolate chips or pieces in a microwave oven or small pan placed over hot but not boiling water. Holding the leaf by the stem, "paint" the *underside* of the leaf with the melted chocolate using a spoon or brush. With your finger, clean off the excess chocolate from both edges of the leaf. Be careful not to get chocolate on the top side of the leaf or it will be difficult to remove the leaf when the chocolate has hardened.

Place the leaves, chocolate side up, on a wax paper-lined dish and refrigerate for 5 to 10 minutes until they are firm. For a curved leaf, place the wet chocolate leaf over a glass or rolling pin to harden in a curved shape. Carefully peel off the leaf from the hardened chocolate.

Chocolate leaves freeze very well so keep them on hand in various sizes to dress up cakes, pies, mousse or any dessert.

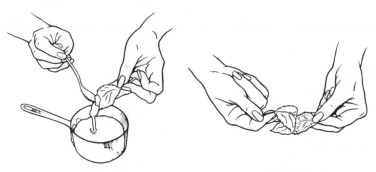

Fig. 1   Fig. 2

Frozen Strawberry Mousse

This eye-catching dessert makes a light but satisfying finale to a full-course dinner. Serve over a pool of Raspberry Sauce (p. 137).

2	egg whites (about ⅓ cup)
¼	cup sugar
1	teaspoon lemon juice
1	10-oz. package frozen strawberries in syrup, thawed
1	tablespoon Kirsch

In a large mixing bowl, warm the egg whites and sugar over another bowl of hot tap water until the sugar dissolves (about 5 minutes).

Beat the egg whites and sugar until foamy, add the lemon juice and continue beating until the whites are very stiff and shiny.

Puree the strawberries and stir in the Kirsch. In a small bowl, stir about one-quarter of the whites into the strawberries, then gently fold the berries into the remaining whites. Line individual soufflé dishes, molds, cupcake pans or custard cups with plastic wrap. Spoon the mixture into the containers and freeze until firm, at least several hours. Makes 3 cups or 4 to 6 servings.

Strawberry Sorbet

This versatile, refreshing treat is perfect to serve as a light dessert, between courses as a palate cleanser, or scooped on top of a Composed Fruit Salad (p. 78). You don't even need an ice cream maker to make this luscious frozen delight.

2	10-oz. packages frozen strawberries in syrup, thawed
2	tablespoons sugar, optional
1	tablespoon lemon juice, optional
1	tablespoon Kirsch, optional

In a food processor bowl or blender, puree the strawberries, sugar, lemon juice and Kirsch. Pour the mixture into a metal cake pan and place it in the freezer.

When the mixture is "slushy" (about 1 hour), return it to the food processor or blender to break up the ice crystals. Pour it back into the cake pan and freeze until the mixture is almost firm.

Scoop the sorbet back into the processor and process again until smooth and fluffy. The color of the mixture will lighten and the volume will increase with each processing.

Pour the sorbet into a freezer container and cover with plastic wrap placed directly on the surface of the sorbet. Refreeze for several hours before serving. Makes about 1 pint.

Toasted Pecan Ice Cream Balls

If you've never had the fun of making a real snowball, here's your chance! The toasted salted pecans give the ice cream a whole new flavor.

**2   cups *Toasted Pecans (p. 46)*
1   quart vanilla ice cream**

Chop the pecans and place them on a piece of wax paper. On another piece of wax paper, drop a 2- to 3-inch diameter scoop of ice cream. Gather up the wax paper around the ice cream and quickly form it into a ball. Drop the ball onto the chopped pecans and quickly roll it to cover it with pecans. Using two forks, transfer the ice cream ball to a piece of plastic wrap, wrap it and place it in the freezer. Repeat this procedure with the remaining ice cream. Makes 8 ice cream balls.

Serve Toasted Pecan Ice Cream Balls over Hot Caramel Apples (p. 134) or on a pool of Hot Fudge Sauce (p. 137).

Idea: Store individually wrapped Toasted Pecan Ice Cream Balls in a large freezer bag or container.

Coconut Almond Ice Cream Balls

**2   cups *Coconut Almond Macaroons (p. 138)*
1   quart vanilla ice cream**

With the food processor or blender running, drop in the macaroons to chop them finely or you can chop them with a knife. Follow the instructions for Toasted Pecan Ice Cream Balls (see above). Makes 8 ice cream balls.

Serve Coconut Almond Ice Cream Balls over the caramel sauce from the Hot Caramel Apples recipe (p. 134) or on a pool of Hot Fudge Sauce (p. 137).

Idea: Make Ice Cream Snowballs by rolling ice cream balls in shredded coconut.

Idea: Make "Tin Roof Sundaes" by rolling ice cream balls in Spanish peanuts and serving them on a pool of Hot Fudge Sauce (p. 137).

Ice Cream Cookie Cups and Cakes

Need a good dessert that's quick, easy and pleasing to all ages? This is the perfect solution.

Cookie Cups
Use your favorite store-bought, cream-filled cookie. One cookie cup takes 3 Oreo-type cookies or 6 filled sugar wafer cookies. (Cookies with double filling hold together better.) Pulverize the cookies in a food processor or blender, or place them in a plastic bag and mash with a rolling pin.

Line a cupcake pan or custard cup with plastic wrap or aluminum foil. Press the crumbs onto the bottom and sides to form a cookie cup. Scoop in ice cream, press down to fill the cookie cup, then top with more cookie crumbs. Wrap well and freeze. Serve plain or drizzle with Hot Fudge Sauce (p. 137).

Cookie Cake
Line a round cake pan with plastic wrap or aluminum foil. Pulverize enough crumbs to cover the bottom and sides of the pan. Press the crumbs firmly into the pan. Fill with softened ice cream, pressing down to fill the cookie cake, then top with a layer of crumbs. Wrap well and freeze. To serve, cut into wedges and drizzle with Hot Fudge Sauce (p. 137).

Idea: Use two flavors of ice cream if you like. Fill the cookie cups or cake halfway with one flavor of ice cream. Freeze until hard, then spread on another flavor of softened ice cream before topping with more cookie crumbs.

 Everyday Hint: When lining a pan with crumbs, place a small plastic bag over your hand to press the crumbs together and form a neat crust.

Butter Pecan Ice Cream

Even expensive gourmet ice cream can't match the full flavor and creamy goodness of homemade ice cream. And you don't need to own an ice cream maker to enjoy this rich and delicious butter pecan.

¼	**cup butter (½ stick)**
1	**cup coarsely chopped pecans**
2	**egg yolks**
1	**14-oz. can sweetened condensed milk (not evaporated milk)**
2	**cups heavy cream**

In a small saucepan over medium heat, melt the butter and stir in the pecans. Stirring constantly, toast the pecans for 3 to 5 minutes until golden brown. The butter should be browned but not burned. Remove from the heat and let cool.

In a medium mixing bowl, beat the egg yolks until they are light and fluffy, then beat in the sweetened condensed milk. (Incorporate as much air as you can into the mixture.) Stir in the butter and pecans.

In another bowl, whip the cream until it forms soft peaks when the beaters are lifted. Gently fold the cream into the egg mixture. Then pour into a metal loaf pan or bowl (metal chills faster than glass), cover with plastic wrap and freeze until firm, at least 5 hours or overnight. Makes about 1 quart.

 Everyday Hint: "Frosty whiskers" form on ice cream and sherbet because air is caught between the container lid and surface of the food. This affects both the quality and flavor of the food. To avoid freezer frost, place plastic wrap directly on the surface of the ice cream.

Best Brownies

Nothing compares with rich, chewy brownies made from scratch. And this recipe wins the best brownie prize hands down.

½	**cup butter (1 stick), melted**
½	**cup sugar**
½	**cup brown sugar**
½	**cup unsweetened cocoa**
2	**eggs**
½	**cup flour**
1	**teaspoon baking powder**
1	**teaspoon vanilla**
½	**cup chopped pecans or walnuts**

Preheat oven to 350 degrees.

In a mixing bowl, beat the butter, sugar, brown sugar and cocoa until well blended. Beat in the eggs, one at a time. Mix the flour and baking powder together, then stir into the cocoa mixture. Stir in the vanilla and nuts. Bake the brownies in a greased or foil-lined 8-inch square cake pan for 25 to 30 minutes until a cake tester or toothpick inserted in center comes out clean. When cool, cut into squares.

Minty Brownies

If you think brownies can't be topped, then you haven't tried these brownies covered with melted peppermint patties.

Make the Best Brownies recipe (see above) or bake brownies from a mix according to package directions. Remove the brownies from the oven and completely cover the hot brownies with chocolate-covered peppermint patties or other chocolate-mint candies that melt easily. Be sure that the mints touch each other. Wait about 5 minutes until the candy softens, then spread the top layer of the chocolate mints to cover the brownies evenly and smooth out the "icing." Chill until the icing is set but not hard, then cut the brownies into squares.

 Everyday Hint: When baking brownies or other bar cookies, line the pan with aluminum foil before baking. The cookies will lift out for easier cutting.

Fruit Bars

Everyone needs a simple yet delicious recipe like this one for emergencies like unexpected company, pot-luck dinners or bake sales.

1	cup butter (2 sticks), softened
1	cup sugar
2	egg yolks
2	cups flour
1	cup chopped nuts
2	10-oz. jars or cans pastry filling (not pie filling), such as apricot, raspberry, date, prune, etc.
	confectioner's sugar

Preheat oven to 325 degrees.

With a mixer, beat the butter until light and fluffy. Gradually beat in the sugar. Beat in the egg yolks, one at a time. Stir in the flour until just mixed, then stir in the nuts.

In a 9 by 13-inch ungreased cake pan, evenly pat three-quarters of the dough to cover the bottom. Spread the filling over the dough. Dot the remaining dough over the filling and pat it down to form an open pattern. Bake for 50 to 55 minutes until the top is golden brown. When cool, sift confectioner's sugar over the top and cut into squares.

Everyday Hint: When patting down cookie dough, wet your hands with cold water to keep the dough from sticking to your hands. The dough will also spread more evenly.

Everyday Hint: Freeze leftover egg whites individually in ice cube trays or Styrofoam egg cartons, then transfer to a freezer bag to have on hand as needed.

Sinfully Rich Chocolate Torte

You can make this impressive chocolate torte using a store-bought pound cake or chocolate cake mix. The real winner is the heavenly Chocolate Buttercream Frosting. It's velvety smooth and incredibly delicious. The hardest part about making it is keeping your fingers out of it.

1	**chocolate cake**
1	**recipe** *Chocolate Buttercream Frosting (see opposite)*

Make your favorite chocolate cake, except bake it in a wax paper-lined jelly roll pan, approx. 15 by 10 by 1 inch. Grease both the pan and the top of the wax paper. Reduce the baking time to just 15 minutes or until a skewer or tester inserted into the center of the cake comes out clean. Do not overbake!

Place the cake in the pan on a cooling rack for 10 minutes so the cake will "set." Place another piece of wax paper over the top of the cake, then place the back of a cookie sheet over the wax paper and invert the cake. Carefully peel off the wax paper from the top of the cake. When thoroughly cool, cut the cake crosswise into 4 equal portions. Slice 2 cake portions in half horizontally (through the 1-inch thickness) to make 4 thin cake layers (see Everyday Hint below). (Use the remaining 2 pieces of cake for another purpose, or make another torte to freeze.)

Spread 1 thin cake layer with buttercream frosting. Top with a second layer and repeat the buttercream and other 2 cake layers. Frost the top and sides of the torte. Reserve some of the frosting for decorations if you like. Use a pastry bag with a star tip to make swirls on the torte.

 Everyday Hint: To slice thin cake layers, encircle the cake with a piece of waxed dental floss long enough to go completely and evenly around the cake. Criss-cross the floss in front of the cake and gently pull both ends of the floss for a perfect slice. If using a pound cake, slice each layer in half again.

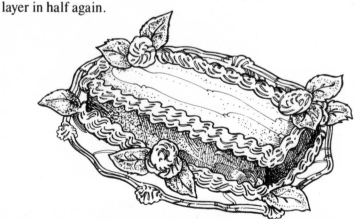

Fig. 1

Chocolate Buttercream Frosting

2	**eggs**
2	**tablespoons water**
1/2	**cup sugar**
1/2	**cup unsweetened cocoa, sifted**
1	**cup butter (2 sticks), softened**
1	**teaspoon vanilla**

In a mixing bowl, warm the eggs, water and sugar over another bowl of hot water until the sugar dissolves (about 5 minutes), stirring occasionally to mix the ingredients. With an electric mixer, beat until the mixture becomes very thick and light and forms a continuous "ribbon" that folds back onto itself when the beaters are lifted. *Do not underbeat.* If using a hand mixer, this may take 5 to 10 minutes. At low speed, stir in the cocoa just until blended.

In another bowl, beat the butter with an electric mixer until it is light and fluffy. Beat the butter into the cocoa mixture a tablespoon at a time, beating well after each addition of butter. (Adding the butter will "deflate" the cocoa mixture.) Add the vanilla and chill slightly for easier spreading. Makes 2 1/2 cups.

 Everyday Hint: Before decorating a frosted cake, place it in the freezer until the frosting is hard. You can correct any mistakes by just scraping off the decorations and starting again. (No one will ever know unless you tell them!)

 Everyday Hint: To freeze a decorated cake, place it in the freezer without any wrapping until the frosting is very hard. (This way the frosting won't stick to the wrapper.) Remove the cake from the freezer, wrap it in airtight freezer wrap then return the cake to the freezer.

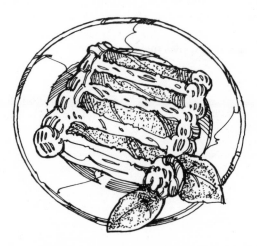

Fig. 2

Hot Caramel Apples

The sweetness of the caramel sauce and the tartness of the apples make this a magic combination. Crowned with a Toasted Pecan Ice Cream Ball (p. 127), this dessert is sheer delight.

4	**large apples (Golden Delicious or Granny Smith)**
1	**tablespoon lemon juice**
½	**cup butter (1 stick)**
½	**cup sugar**
½	**cup heavy cream**
1	**teaspoon cinnamon**

Peel, core and cut the apples into ½-inch wedges. Place them in a bowl and sprinkle with lemon juice.

In a large skillet, melt the butter over high heat. Add the sugar, stirring constantly, until the mixture just turns golden brown. This takes only a minute so don't let it burn. Pour in the cream and cinnamon, stirring vigorously for 2 minutes until the mixture thickens and looks like caramel.

Add the apples and stir to coat with caramel. Cover the pan, reduce the heat and simmer for about 5 minutes until the apples are just tender. (Test apples for doneness with a toothpick.) Don't overcook them; they should not be mushy.

With a slotted spoon, transfer the apples to a bowl and set aside. Over high heat, bring the caramel to a boil again and stir for about 2 minutes until thickened. Pour the caramel over the apples.

To serve, spoon the apples into individual serving bowls. Place a scoop of vanilla ice cream, Butter Pecan Ice Cream (p. 129) or a Toasted Pecan Ice Cream Ball (p. 127) over the apples. Top with Cinnamon Whipped Cream (p. 160). Makes at least 6 servings.

Idea: Serve Hot Caramel Apples over Pastry Shells (p. 156), waffles or pancakes.

 Everyday Hint: Mix cinnamon with an equal amount of sugar before stirring it into a liquid so that the cinnamon is incorporated evenly and doesn't lump together or float on top.

Sicilian Cassata

This traditional Sicilian favorite—"cassata" means cream cake in Italian—boasts layers of flavorful sweetened ricotta cheese, chocolate and almonds covered with luscious chocolate frosting.

1	baked pound cake (store-bought or homemade)
2	cups ricotta cheese (15-oz. carton)
2	tablespoons heavy cream
½	cup confectioner's sugar
3	tablespoons orange-flavored liqueur (Cointreau, Grand Marnier, Strega)
¼	teaspoon cinnamon
¼	cup slivered almonds
½	cup semi-sweet chocolate chips or pieces (3 ounces)
1	recipe *Chocolate Buttercream Frosting (p. 133)* or your favorite chocolate frosting almonds for garnish

With a serrated knife or dental floss (see Everyday Hint p. 132), cut the cake horizontally into four thin layers.

In a bowl, beat the cheese, cream, sugar, liqueur and cinnamon until thoroughly combined. Stir in the almonds and chocolate.

Place the bottom layer of cake on a piece of aluminum foil large enough to cover the cake. Spread the layer generously with the cheese mixture. Cover with another cake layer and repeat, ending with a plain layer of cake on top. Wrap the cake in the aluminum foil and refrigerate for at least 3 hours until the cheese is firm.

Frost the top and sides of the cassata and sprinkle with almonds.

Refrigerate the cake uncovered until the frosting is firm.

Cover the frosted cake with plastic wrap and refrigerate for at least a day before serving, to allow the flavors to mellow and blend.

Poached Pears

Served plain or in a pool of raspberry or chocolate sauce, poached pears provide a light, refreshing finish to any meal.

2½	**cups water**
½	**cup sugar**
¼	**lemon, or 2 teaspoons lemon juice**
2	**cinnamon sticks**
2	**whole cloves**
1	**teaspoon vanilla**
6	**firm pears with stems**

In a saucepan just large enough for 6 pears to fit standing upright, mix together the water, sugar, lemon quarter, cinnamon sticks, cloves and vanilla. Cover, bring the mixture to a boil and simmer for 15 minutes.

Peel the pears. With a corer or small paring knife, carefully core each pear from the bottom, leaving the stem intact. Cut a thin slice from the bottom so the pears stand up straight. Arrange the pears in the poaching syrup, cover the pan and poach until the pears are just tender. This will take about 5 to 20 minutes depending on the type and ripeness of the pears. Test with a toothpick for doneness. (Don't overcook the pears. You don't want them to be mushy.) Remove from the heat and allow the pears to cool in the syrup. Refrigerate the pears in the syrup until thoroughly chilled. (Poached pears will keep for several days.)

To serve, place each pear on a pool of Hot Fudge Sauce (p. 137) or Raspberry Sauce (p. 137), or serve plain. Serve poached pears with a knife and fork for easy eating. With a sauce, you'll need a spoon to get every last drop. Makes 6 servings.

 Everyday Hint: When peeling pears, apples or peaches, cover with water and lemon juice to keep the fruit from turning brown.

Hot Fudge Sauce

This sauce is as quick and easy as it is delicious. Keep it as a staple in the refrigerator but label it "Stewed Prunes" or it will never be there when you need it!

1/2	cup butter (1 stick)
1	cup semi-sweet chocolate chips or pieces (6 ounces)
1	13-oz. can evaporated milk
1 1/2	cups sifted confectioner's sugar
1	teaspoon vanilla

In a saucepan, melt the butter and chocolate over low heat. Stir in the evaporated milk and sugar, then bring the mixture to a boil while continuing to stir. Lower the heat to simmer and stir for 3 to 5 minutes until the sauce has thickened. Remove the pan from the heat and stir in the vanilla. The sauce will thicken as it cools. Serve hot or cold. Makes 2 cups.

Raspberry Sauce

Nothing says simple elegance better than serving poached pears or a scoop of ice cream in a pool of this brilliant red sauce brimming with exquisite raspberry flavor.

1	10-oz. package frozen raspberries (or strawberries) in syrup, thawed
1	tablespoon cornstarch
1/2	teaspoon lemon juice
1/4	teaspoon cinnamon
1	teaspoon butter
1	teaspoon Kirsch, optional

Drain the syrup from the raspberries and set the berries aside.

In a small saucepan over medium-high heat, combine the raspberry syrup, cornstarch, lemon juice and cinnamon. Bring the mixture to a boil, stirring constantly for several minutes, until it is thick and clear. Remove from the heat and stir in the butter and Kirsch. Cool the sauce slightly, stir in the reserved berries and chill. Makes 1 cup.

Chocolate Pears with Macaroon Filling

For those of us who think fruit is fine but dessert is chocolate, here is a perfect solution. The crunchy macaroon filling inside the tender pear is a pleasant surprise.

1	**cup semi-sweet chocolate chips or pieces (6 ounces)**
¼	**cup butter (½ stick)**
6	***Poached Pears (p. 136),* cored from the bottom**
	***Coconut Almond Macaroons (see below),* crumbled**

In a small saucepan over very low heat, melt the chocolate and butter together and then let cool slightly. Drain the poached pears and pat them dry with paper towels. Carefully fill each cored pear bottom with crumbled macaroons. Holding it by the stem, spoon warm chocolate over the pear, coating it completely and allowing the excess chocolate to drain off. Place the pears on a dish until the chocolate is set. Keep the pears at room temperature until serving time because refrigeration may cause the chocolate to sweat.

Top each pear with a fresh mint leaf or garnish with a Chocolate Leaf (p. 125). Makes 6 servings.

Coconut Almond Macaroons

Crispy on the outside and chewy on the inside, these macaroons freeze beautifully and thaw quickly. It's almost like having a cookie jar in your freezer.

1	**14-oz. bag sweetened coconut, or 2 7-oz. cans**
1½	**cups almonds, sliced or slivered**
½	**cup flour**
1	**14-oz. can sweetened condensed milk (not evaporated milk)**
2	**tablespoons butter, melted**
2	**teaspoons vanilla**

Preheat oven to 300 degrees.

In a large bowl, mix the coconut, almonds and flour. Stir together the sweetened condensed milk, melted butter and vanilla, then mix well with the coconut mixture. Drop heaping teaspoons of batter onto a well-buttered baking sheet.

Bake for 20 to 25 minutes until golden brown. Immediately remove the macaroons from the baking sheet to cooling racks. Makes about 4 dozen.

Idea: Crumble or chop Coconut Almond Macaroons and fold into sweetened whipped cream. Serve over sliced strawberries, raspberries, peaches or seedless grapes.

Shortcake

When berries or peaches are in season, there's nothing better than the simple pleasure of tender shortcake heaped with fresh fruit and covered with whipped cream.

1	recipe *Basic Biscuit Mix (p. 25)*
2	tablespoons sugar
¾	cup half-and-half cream
	fresh or frozen berries or fruit

Preheat oven to 425 degrees.

In a bowl, combine the Basic Biscuit Mix and sugar. Pour in the half-and-half cream and stir with a fork until the dry ingredients are just moistened and the dough begins to chase itself around the bowl. Do not overmix! Turn the dough out onto a lightly floured surface and press together.

To knead, fold the top half of the dough toward you. Using the palms of your hands, gently push the dough away from you. Then turn the dough a quarter turn. Repeat this fold, push, turn procedure 8 to 10 times or until the dough just holds together. If the dough seems too sticky, add a little more flour.

With a rolling pin, gently roll the dough from the center out until it is ½ inch thick. With a floured 3- to 4-inch round cutter cut circles as closely together as possible. Place them 2 inches apart on an ungreased baking sheet. Press together (do not knead) the remaining scraps of dough and cut again. Bake for 8 to 12 minutes until lightly browned.

To serve, split each shortcake in half. Place the bottom half in a bowl or plate and spoon on berries or fruit. Top with remaining shortcake, more fruit and whipped cream or ice cream. Makes about 8 shortcakes.

Fruit Cobbler

With Basic Biscuit Mix and canned pie filling on hand, this homey and wonderfully satisfying dessert is oven-ready in minutes.

1	**21-oz. can fruit pie filling (cherry, peach, apple, blueberry, etc.)**
1	**tablespoon lemon juice**
¼	**teaspoon cinnamon**
1	**recipe** *Basic Biscuit Mix* **(p. 25)**
2	**tablespoons sugar**
1	**cup milk**

Preheat oven to 400 degrees.

Combine the pie filling, lemon juice and cinnamon and pour into a buttered 8- or 9-inch round or square baking pan. In a bowl, combine the Basic Biscuit Mix and sugar. Pour in the milk and stir with a fork just until the dry ingredients are moistened. Do not overmix! Drop spoonfuls of the batter over the fruit to cover it. Bake for 25 minutes until the top is lightly browned. Serve warm.

Idea: Top cobbler with a scoop of ice cream or serve with a small pitcher of cream to pour over it.

Idea: Sprinkle Streusel Topping (p. 117) over biscuit dough before baking.

Everyday Hint: Baking powder causes quick breads to rise, first when it comes in contact with the liquid, and again when it is heated during the baking. Always store baking powder in a tightly covered container and check it for freshness by mixing a teaspoon of it with a small amount of water. If bubbles do not form, don't use it.

Everyday Hint: Canned fruit pie fillings taste much more like fresh fruit if you add lemon juice and cinnamon.

Apricot Soufflé

Not too sweet, not too tart, this delicately colored and flavored soufflé can be made hours ahead, refrigerated and baked just before serving.

1	**12-oz. jar or can apricot pastry filling (not pie filling)**
1	**tablespoon lemon juice**
6	**egg whites (1 cup)**
1/3	**cup sugar**
	confectioner's sugar

Preheat oven to 375 degrees.

Butter and sugar 6 individual ½-cup custard cups or soufflé molds. Refrigerate molds until ready to fill.

In a bowl, mix the apricot filling and lemon juice. Set aside.

In a large mixing bowl, warm the egg whites and sugar over hot water for about 5 minutes until the sugar dissolves. Beat the egg whites and sugar until they form very stiff peaks when the beaters are lifted. Beat 1 cup of the egg whites into the apricots, then lightly fold the mixture into the whites.

Spoon the soufflé mixture into the prepared molds, mounding the mixture about 1 inch above the rims and forming the tops into cone shapes.

Place the soufflés in a baking pan and place in the oven. Pour boiling water into the pan to reach halfway up the sides of the molds. Bake for 25 minutes.

With a metal spatula, remove the soufflés from the water bath and sift confectioner's sugar over the tops. Place the soufflé dishes on plates and serve immediately. Makes 6 servings.

Chocolate Truffles

These are the ultimate chocolate experience. Chocolate truffles are very rich, so don't make them too big. Remember... one who indulges—bulges.

2	cups semi-sweet chocolate chips or pieces (12 ounces)
¼	cup unsalted butter (½ stick), cut in pieces
1	cup heavy cream
1	tablespoon liqueur (Cognac, Grand Marnier, Chambord, Amaretto, etc.), optional
1	cup chopped nuts, optional
	cocoa powder, unsweetened

Put the chocolate and butter in a blender or food processor. Heat the cream until little bubbles form around the edge, but do not boil. With the machine running, pour in the hot cream, then the liqueur. Blend just until smooth. Stir in chopped nuts by hand. Pour the chocolate mixture into a shallow pan and freeze until firm.

Sift cocoa onto wax paper. Using a small scoop or two spoons, scoop out the frozen chocolate and drop onto the cocoa. Dust your hands with the cocoa and lightly roll the truffles into a rough ball 1 inch in diameter. (They melt fast so work quickly. If they get too soft, return the pan to the freezer.)

Roll the truffles in more cocoa and place them in candy papers or miniature muffin papers. Store them in the refrigerator or freezer. Makes 36 truffles.

Idea: Roll truffles in finely chopped nuts instead of more cocoa, or dip frozen truffles in melted chocolate to coat.

Candy Turtles

Here's one turtle that won't be slow to go! When you serve these scrumptious chocolate-covered pecan treats, they're sure to be snapped up as quickly as you can make them.

20	***Toasted Pecans (p. 46)***
8	**caramels**
1	**ounce milk chocolate or semi-sweet chocolate**

To microwave: Line a flat dish with wax paper. Arrange 5 pecan halves to form the turtle's head and feet. Place two caramels on top of the pecans. Microwave 4 turtles on high power for 10 to 20 seconds to soften the caramels. With the back of a spoon, press the caramels into the pecans to form the turtle's shell. Microwave the chocolate in a small bowl on high power for 1½ minutes. Spread the chocolate over the caramel. Chill the turtles until the chocolate is hardened. Makes 4 turtles.

To oven bake: Follow the microwave instructions, except arrange the pecans and caramels on an aluminum foil-lined baking sheet and bake in a 300 degree oven for 5 to 8 minutes until the caramels soften.

Fig. 1

Fig. 2

Fig. 3

Fig. 4

When Company Comes

People offer all sorts of excuses as to why they can't have company over for dinner, and they're all just that—excuses. "My house isn't nice enough" is one popular excuse. Yet some of the loveliest meals I can remember have been given in very modest homes where the simplest fare was served with the same loving care and devotion that the family felt for one another and everyone who entered their home. Those memorable meals nurtured both body and soul. Good food and good feelings depend more on the cook than the pocketbook.

If you are concerned about the appearance of your home, there are many inexpensive, cosmetic things that can be done to spruce up the place and make it more festive. Adding some new houseplants will give you and the house a lift. Decorative throw pillows can tie a room together, update a color scheme and provide extra floor seating if a crowd is coming. For the bathroom, get some new hand towels if you need them and perhaps a new throw rug. Put out fresh bars of soap and any toiletries that your guests might need and freshen the room with flowers or a scented candle.

The real reason many people avoid entertaining is just plain old fear of failure. But when you entertain the easy everyday gourmet way, your party can be as much fun for you as it is for your guests.

There's a wonderful exhilaration and excitement that goes with entertaining. But it's the planning and advance preparation that determines how much you will enjoy your own party. To enjoy it, you've got to be relaxed and free of last-minute details. The best way I know to do that is to make detailed lists of all the jobs that have to be done before the party.

If entertaining is new to you, keep it small and simple. Invite people that you feel comfortable with—perhaps just one other person or another couple. Or you might choose to give a party with a friend. It can be double the fun and half the work and expense. Sharing a party is especially appealing when you want to entertain more people than you can handle easily by yourself.

Just remember that the most important thing is for you and your company to have a good time. For centuries people have been breaking bread together as a sign of their friendship and love for one another. Whether it's to celebrate a special occasion or just to share a meal, the real purpose is to enjoy your guests—not to impress them.

Decide what kind of occasion your party will be and where you will entertain. Whether it's to be dinner in the dining room, kitchen or living room will determine your overall menu and serving plans. Check to see what dishes and serving pieces you have, since this may limit your menu choices.

How you plan to serve your guests will also affect your menu. If you prefer buffet style, select foods that can be eaten without using a knife. It's too difficult to balance a plate while trying to cut a large piece of meat.

When choosing your menu, keep in mind the season, your budget and dishes that you are familiar with. Do try out some new recipes but make sure you have a good idea how the dish should look and taste, or prepare it for yourself or your family ahead of time so that you will feel more confident. Using the recipes in this book, I've put together some menus for different occasions with a food preparation schedule for each. You may wish to use them as a guide (p. 162).

When you have selected your menu, write down everything that has to be done for each dish. (If you can, photocopy the recipes you'll be using to make your grocery list; it's much easier than juggling cookbooks.) Mark what to do ahead and check off jobs as they are completed. Make note of which serving dishes and garnishing ideas to use.

A good host or hostess anticipates the needs and wishes of guests. That's why a "dry run" is a good idea. Set the table or buffet ahead of time and review each portion of the meal to be sure you haven't forgotten anything. It's not a big deal even if you have, but you will be calmer and your guests will be more relaxed if you aren't bobbing up and down throughout the meal.

It's fun to plan a party around a theme—like a Spring Brunch with lots of pastel colors and spring flowers, or maybe a Winter Indoor Picnic served in individual napkin-lined baskets full of goodies for everyone. Your menu can set the theme—an Italian dinner served buffet style. Or let an event like the Super Bowl dictate a party's direction.

Your table can carry out your theme. An inexpensive and versatile way to have an elegant table covering is to place a see-through fabric over a colorful cloth. If you buy sheer, wide drapery fabric and colored bed sheets, you don't even have to sew a seam. Just by changing the undercloth, you can have a different color scheme for any occasion all year round.

Candles always add to the specialness of an occasion. Don't worry about matching candleholders—a cluster of candlesticks of different heights and shapes can be attractive and innovative. Double the candlelight by arranging the candles on a mirror. And a mirror image of your centerpiece adds a whimsical yet elegant note to any table setting or buffet.

You can buy expensive bevel-edged mirrors for your table, or you can get the same effect with an inexpensive door mirror from a hardware or discount department store. Glue some felt pieces to the underside of the mirror so it won't scratch the table. A mirror on a serving table also protects it against spills and hot dishes.

Fresh flowers are always a treat, but instead of one large centerpiece, make little individual bouquets for each placesetting. You don't need matching vases—any small containers, even baby food jars, will do. Dress up the containers with colorful ribbons that match the table covering; repeat the ribbon as a napkin ring holding a flower. Matching ribbon looped through the bouquets and around the table will add a unifying and finishing touch to the table.

Chocolate Placecards

Chocolate placecards are a knock-out way to get any party or special dinner off to a great start. And when they're chocolate, you can have your placecards and eat them, too!

Make chocolate placecards by using two chocolate squares, chocolate mint squares or any small chocolate bar. Join the chocolate pieces together by slightly melting the edges. Heat an empty pan, touch one side of each chocolate square to the hot pan for just a second until the chocolate starts to soften. On a piece of wax paper, place the chocolates face down and lightly push the melted edges together.

To prop up the placecard, cut another chocolate square in half diagonally to make two triangles. Soften one of the short sides of each triangle and attach to the back of the placecard at each end. Chill them for about 5 minutes until the chocolate is firm.

For easy decorating, line up the placecards on a raised cooling rack, face side up. Write the names with tubes of decorating icing or use store-bought candy letters and glue on with icing.

Decorate the placecard edges to go with your holiday or party theme. Using icing as a base, attach colored sprinkles or candies. Put the placecard on a small doily at each placesetting.

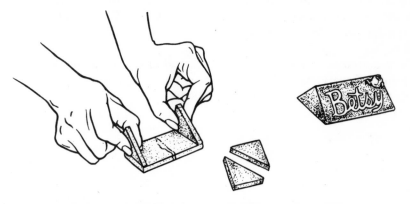

Fig. 1   Fig. 2

Beverages

It's hospitable to offer your guests a beverage before dinner. Whether it contains alcohol or not is your decision. You may choose to set up a special place for drinks and let your guests help themselves. Have everything on hand—ice bucket, ice server, glasses, lemon peel, stirrers, small napkins, etc.

Kir Royale

Before dinner, I like to offer one special drink—that way I don't have to play bartender. A very pleasant drink is Kir, which is chilled white wine mixed with a fruit-flavored liqueur. Instead of white wine, used chilled Champagne for an even more special Kir Royale. This one is layered by using a funnel trick. As you drink the Kir, the flavors blend.

6	ounces Champagne, well chilled
1	ounce berry-flavored liqueur such as Chambord, Cassis or Cranberry (2 tablespoons)
1	raspberry or strawberry (fresh or individually frozen)

Just before serving, pour the chilled Champagne into a large, stemmed wine glass. Place a funnel into the center of the glass until it touches the bottom. Drizzle the liqueur down the funnel into the bottom of the glass and then slowly lift the funnel to remove it. Drop a berry into the Champagne and serve immediately. Makes 1 drink.

Idea: If you prefer to serve no alcohol at all, substitute Grenadine syrup for the liqueur and sparkling white grape juice or sparkling apple juice for the Champagne. Both are available at grocery stores.

Ice Tricks

Automatic ice cube makers are great, but don't throw away those old ice cube trays—they're perfect for making decorative flavored ice cubes. Styrofoam or plastic egg cartons work fine, too.

Use leftover beverages to make ice cubes for your favorite iced drinks. If you make cubes from vegetable juice, fruit juice, coffee or tea, the flavor won't dilute as the ice melts. When serving iced tea, make frozen cubes of lemon juice or lemonade to take the place of fresh lemon wedges—without the seeds.

Make plain drinks look pretty by filling ice cubes with fruits or vegetables. For sweet drinks try cherries, berries, pineapple chunks, orange sections or mint leaves frozen right into the cube. Spice up savory drinks with cubes filled with olives, pearl onions, lemon or lime twists. Freeze fruits or vegetables in juices that are compatible with the drink.

When preparing beverages by the pitcherful, make larger cubes in cupcake pans because they melt more slowly. Dip the bottom of the pan in warm water to release the cubes.

Make ice rings for punch bowls by freezing water or juice in a ring mold, bundt pan or round cake pan. To decorate the ice ring, fill the ring mold with $1/2$- to 1-inch liquid and arrange the fruit, mint leaves, etc., in a design in the liquid. Freeze until very hard, then add the remaining liquid that has been thoroughly chilled. Freeze. Dip the bottom of the pan in warm water to release the ring. Invert the ring into the punch bowl. (Be sure that the size of the ice ring fits into the punch bowl and still allows space for the punch ladle. Also, make the ring small enough to fit in the bowl as the level of the punch drops.)

Make ice cubes and rings ahead of time and store them in plastic freezer bags until ready to use.

 Everyday Hint: To expand refrigerator space for a party, buy bags of ice to fill clean ice chests or coolers. Store beverages or other bulky items and extra ice cubes in the coolers.

 Everyday Hint: For clearer ice when making decorative ice cubes or rings, use distilled water or water that has been boiled and then chilled.

Appetizers and Starters

It's always nice to have a little something to nibble on as your friends are arriving. You'll want to serve something that's tasty but not filling, and the flavor shouldn't be overpowering. Choose a savory starter to stimulate the appetite rather than a sweet one that might suppress it. Hot Toasted Pecans (p. 46) make an ideal starter. Instead of serving the nuts in one large dish, place several small dishes around the room so everyone can get some.

For casual get togethers, serve finger foods so people can munch and mingle. But for the sake of your guests and your carpet, provide napkins and small plates.

Vegetable Tree

Raw vegetables make a great snack or party food, but they'll taste even better if they're cooked for just a few minutes to bring out the color and flavor of the vegetables and make them tender-crisp. (See blanching instructions and list of vegetables that should be blanched on p. 34). Instead of just a platter of veggies, show off a little and make a Vegetable Tree.

> **Styrofoam cone, at least 12 inches tall**
> **plastic wrap**
> **wooden toothpicks**
> **U-shaped craft pins, optional**
> **endive or other curly greens**
> **assorted vegetables**

Cover the Styrofoam cone with plastic wrap. Starting at the base of the cone, attach the endive with toothpicks or U-shaped craft pins to completely cover the cone. Clean the vegetables and cut them into bite-sized pieces. Vary the vegetable shapes by cutting them with cookie cutters or a ripple-edged knife if you desire. Blanch the vegetables, refresh them in cold water, then dry them thoroughly. The vegetables can be prepared the day before and stored in plastic bags with a paper towel inside to absorb excess moisture.

Spear the vegetables with toothpicks and attach them to the cone starting at the base. Form spirals, rows, stripes or a design of your choice. Lightly sprinkle water over the Vegetable Tree and wrap it with plastic wrap to preserve its freshness. Refrigerate the tree until ready to serve. The Vegetable Tree can be assembled hours ahead of time. Serve it with Herb Mayonnaise Dip (p. 36), Hot Spinach Cheese Dip (p. 36) or any other dip.

The combination of vegetables I like to use for a tree is:

First spiral: Whole cherry tomatoes.

Second spiral: Alternate cauliflower florets with carrots that have been sliced diagonally, ¼ inch thick. Attach the carrots so that they extend out between the pieces of cauliflower.

Third spiral: With a ripple-edged cutter, cut yellow squash into slices ½ inch thick, then cut them in half crosswise and attach the squash to the cone with the rounded side out. Alternate the squash with radishes that have been cut like a "mum" (p. 35).

Attach the vegetables to the cone so that each spiral goes around the cone twice. Place the Vegetable Tree on a large serving platter and arrange additional vegetables around the base of the tree along with the dips.

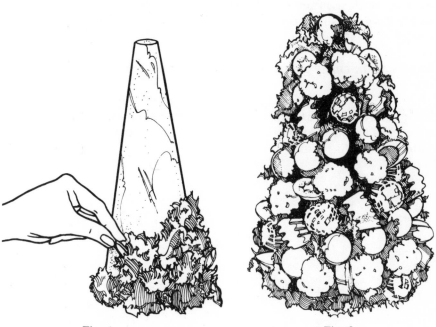

Fig. 1   Fig. 2

Stuffed Cheese Wheel

Everybody loves a cheese ball, and it looks gorgeous until the first person cuts into it. But messiness isn't a problem when cheese is served in its own shell.

1   **2-pound cheddar cheese wheel encased in red or black wax (or Gouda or Edam cheese)**

Cut a circle about ½ inch in from the top edge of the wax casing. Remove the circle and, with a knife or spoon, hollow out the cheese, leaving the shell intact and about ¼ inch of the cheese on the insides and bottom of the wax casing.

Use the cheese for making Savory Cheddar Cheese Spread (p. 30) or other cheese spreads. Stuff the wheel with the cheese mixture and sprinkle the top with chopped nuts. Chill the wheel.

Remove the cheese from the refrigerator 30 minutes before serving so the cheese has a spreadable consistency. Refill the wheel with more cheese as needed.

Idea: Save the empty cheese casing container and freeze it to use another time.

Idea: For a decorative touch, cut V-shaped notches or scallops around the top edge of the cheese wheel. Use a star or scalloped cookie cutter as a pattern.

Garnishing and Presentation

If food looks good, you've already won over the people you're feeding. Small finishing touches can make the difference between a plate looking so-so or sensational. When serving food with a sauce, present the food over the sauce instead of hiding it underneath. Arrange vegetables attractively or choose two vegetables that complement each other in color and flavor. Instead of tossing a salad, compose it to balance the shapes and colors. If appropriate, try using fruits or vegetables as containers for other foods. Bake meat in a puff pastry wrapping or serve it on a pastry shell.

Frosted Grapes

Frosted grapes are delicious and impressive as a snack, appetizer or dessert, and they make a beautiful, edible garnish. Use either red or green grapes, but make sure they're seedless.

2	pounds seedless grapes, red or green
1	egg white
1	tablespoon water
1	cup sugar

Wash, dry and separate the grapes into small clusters. Lightly beat the egg white with the water until it is frothy.

Dip the grape clusters into the egg white, letting the excess drain back into the bowl, then place them on wax paper until all the grape clusters are dipped. Allow the grapes to dry for a few minutes until they are "tacky."

Place the sugar on a plate or wax paper and roll the grapes in the sugar to coat them completely. Place the Frosted Grapes in the refrigerator for at least 1 hour, uncovered, to chill and harden the sugar. Serve them cold. Frosted Grapes can be made several days in advance and kept in the refrigerator.

Idea: Frosted Grapes freeze well and are delicious and refreshing served directly from the freezer.

Fruit Baskets

Fruit Baskets are a very attractive way to serve fruit or desserts. Use smaller fruits (oranges, grapefruit, small melons) for individual servings and side dishes; use larger ones (watermelons or other large melons) for serving a crowd.

Grapefruit Basket
Cut off the top third of a grapefruit and carefully hollow out the inside, removing all of the fruit with a pointed spoon. To form double handles, make a slice ¼ inch in from each side of the grapefruit, almost to the center. Lift and tie the handles together with a thin strip of grapefruit peel or a ribbon. Fill the basket with grapefruit, orange and kiwi fruit slices.

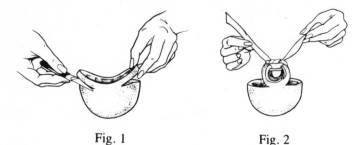

Fig. 1   Fig. 2

Lemon Basket
To form the handle, make two cuts, ¼ inch apart, to the center on the same long side of a lemon. Cut in from each end to meet the first two cuts and remove the wedge-shaped pieces. Scoop out the pulp with a pointed spoon. If you like, carve V-shaped wedges around the top of the basket using scissors or a knife. Fill the lemon basket with cranberry sauce or any condiment.

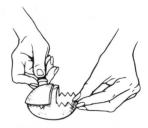

Watermelon Basket

Cut off the top third of a watermelon, hollow it out and make melon balls. Using a small star cookie cutter, punch out stars from the leftover rind. (A rubber mallet from the hardware store makes the job easier.)

With toothpicks, secure the stars around the melon edge. Alternate honeydew and watermelon stars for an attractive effect. Fill the melon basket with melon balls and other fruit.

Paper Frills

Paper Frills are a great way to dress up chicken drumsticks or drumettes. They can also be used for Cornish hens, chops, turkey or the shank bone of a ham.

To make frills for chicken legs, fold a standard 8½ by 11-inch piece of paper in half crosswise and cut along the fold. Then fold each piece of paper in half again (each piece of folded paper is now 8½ by 2¾ inches).

With scissors, make cuts ⅛-inch apart through the fold to about 1 inch from the open sides. Turn the paper inside out so the frills will be nice and full. Wrap the uncut edges of the paper around your fingers and secure the ends with a piece of tape. Slip the frills over the bone just before serving.

Idea: Vary the paper size when making paper frills for other meats. For turkey or ham frills use a full 8½ by 11-inch piece of paper folded in half lengthwise. For Cornish hens or chicken drumettes, use a 4 by 4-inch piece of paper folded in half.

Idea: Color coordinate frills with your tablesetting by using colored paper.

Idea: Make frills out of aluminum foil when cooking for a crowd. They can be shaped right onto the legs before baking to save last-minute fussing.

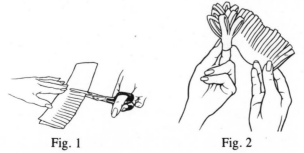

Fig. 1   Fig. 2

Shell Pastry

With these unique pastry shells, you can easily turn a routine main dish or dessert into a very special event.

1   **recipe pie dough (enough for a 9-inch pie)**
8   **scallop shells, approximately 5 inches across (2 for each pastry
         shell)**

Preheat oven to 350 degrees.

Roll out the pie dough into a 10-inch circle, 1/8 inch thick, and divide it into four pieces. Place one piece of the dough over the outside of a lightly greased scallop shell. Gently shape the dough over the shell.

Using a knife, trim the excess dough from all around the edge of the shell. Lightly grease the inside of another scallop shell that is about the same size and place it on top of the pastry to hold it in place while baking. Place the pastry and shells on a baking sheet with the rounded sides of the shells up.

Bake for 20 minutes, remove the top shell and continue to bake for 5 minutes or until golden brown. Let the pastry cool on the shells before carefully removing.

Keep a supply of baked pastry shells in the freezer. Use them to hold desserts or any recipe that you would serve over noodles or rice or with a sauce. Makes 4 shells.

 Everyday Hint: When shaping pastry dough into or over a mold or pan, use a small ball of dough scraps to help press the pastry dough into place. This helps to shape the dough and prevents it from tearing and stretching.

Pastry Rose

This edible masterpiece can be made with leftover scraps of dough. Top your next pie with a pastry rose and I'll guarantee you'll be a blooming success.

Using homemade or store-bought pie dough or dough scraps, cut 4 pastry circles the same size (3 to 4 inches in diameter) and stack them.

With your thumbs under the center of the stack, pull the edges of the dough down to form a ball. Pinch all the edges together and hold them in one hand.

With a sharp knife, cut an "X" through the center of the dough ball, carefully cutting through all four layers of dough. With the tip of the knife, carefully separate the "petals" and unfold them to make the rose "bloom."

Place the rose in the center of an unbaked, two-crust pie or other unbaked pastry. Cut three pastry leaves out of leftover dough. With the back of a knife, score the leaves lightly to form the veins. Arrange the leaves around the base of the rose, twisting the leaves a little so they look more natural.

If you wish, lightly brush the top of the pie, rose petals and leaves with an egg wash (1 egg beaten with 1 tablespoon water) before baking to give a golden finish to the crust.

Idea: Make Pastry Roses out of any type of dough—puff pastry, pie pastry, yeast dough, etc.

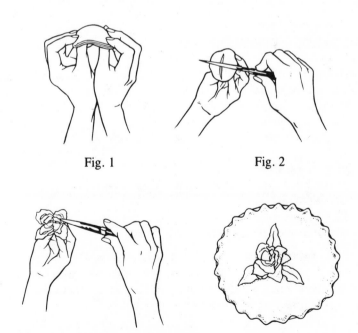

Fig. 1   Fig. 2

Fig. 3   Fig. 4

Serving

If dinner is presented family style where guests help themselves, a sprig or sprinkling of fresh herbs might enhance the platter, or you might surround the main dish with cherry tomatoes or Stuffin' Muffins (p. 119).

For buffet-style dinners, arrange food in the order that it should be placed on the plate—gravy or sauces next to the foods they're meant to go with. Place flowers or candles to the back or sides of the serving table so guests won't knock them over or have to reach around them.

Serving dinner on individual plates gives you the perfect opportunity to be creative. You can arrange the plates in the kitchen and ask someone else to help you serve them. Just be sure to tell your helper to serve the plates with the "green beans on the bottom right" if you want to preserve your artwork. Don't forget to wipe off any drops or smears from around the plate before you serve it. No matter what type of service you choose, heat the plates beforehand so the food doesn't get cold as quickly.

Dessert

Our last memory of any meal is dessert, so make it memorable and the crowning glory of your efforts. Most desserts can be made in advance, giving you the advantage of a flexible time schedule. You can make your old "stand-by" dessert and dress it up with Chocolate Leaves (p. 125). Or if the season is right, you can't beat this Chocolate Strawberry Tree.

Chocolate Strawberry Tree

This spectacular and incredibly delicious creation never fails to get oohs and aahs. My good friend and colleague Elaine Gonzalez, chocolate specialist and author of the excellent book **Chocolate Artistry** *(by Contemporary Books), showed me how to construct it. I was amazed at how easily and quickly it could be made, since it's such a masterpiece.*

4 to 6	**pints fresh strawberries**
2	**pounds milk, semi-sweet or white candy-making chocolate (see Note opposite)**
1	**12-inch Styrofoam cone wax paper or plastic wrap**

The number of strawberries needed will be determined by their size. If they are clean with no sand or dirt fragments, then you don't have to wash them. If not, rinse them quickly under running water and dry them completely with paper towels before dipping them into the chocolate.

On a paper towel-lined tray or flat surface, line up the berries according to size from the largest to the smallest. Set aside a perfect berry for the top of the tree.

Cover the Styrofoam cone tightly with wax paper or plastic wrap and secure it with tape. Set the cone on a serving platter.

Melt the chocolate coating over very low heat or microwave it according to your microwave oven directions.

Begin the first row of berries at the bottom of the cone, using the largest berries first. Grasp a berry by the stem and dip it halfway into the melted chocolate coating. Immediately position it against the base of the cone with the pointed end of the berry down. Continue dipping and placing the berries touching each other side-by-side around the base of the cone. The chocolate coating will harden quickly, securing the berries to the wax paper and each other.

For the second row, position the points of the berries in between the tops of the berries in the row below. Continue dipping and forming rows of strawberries all the way to the top of the cone. It is usually not necessary to chill the cone as you work, but if the chocolate softens because the room is too warm, chill the cone briefly and then continue. (It is not necessary to refrigerate the tree once assembled.)

Idea: Surround the Chocolate Strawberry Tree with additional chocolate-dipped berries to be eaten first.

Idea: Make Chocolate Leaves (p. 125) to accent the berries and fill out any empty spaces between them, or arrange the chocolate leaves at the base of the tree.

Idea: "Double dip" the berries. Dip them first in melted white chocolate candy coating. Place on wax paper to let the white chocolate dry and set, then dip the berries into either milk or dark chocolate covering all but $1/4$ inch of the white chocolate so both colors are visible. After the second dipping, place the berries directly onto the cone and proceed to make the Chocolate Strawberry Tree.

Idea: Make chocolate-dipped berries or other fruits in smaller quantities to serve anytime. Place them directly on a serving plate or in individual candy papers or miniature muffin paper liners.

Note: I recommend chocolate-flavored coating for dipping berries or other fruit. It is also called compound coating, confectioner's coating or summer coating and is about half the cost of "real" chocolate. Since chocolate coating does not contain cocoa butter, it doesn't melt as quickly and doesn't need the special "tempering" treatment required of "real" chocolate. It can be purchased in pellet or wafer form at craft stores, candy-making supply stores and most supermarkets.

After Dinner

Many people enjoy coffee with dessert after dinner. There are many exotic blends (with exotic price tags) that can be purchased in specialty shops, but you can add an easy, everyday gourmet touch that only tastes expensive. Stir ½ teaspoon cinnamon into your everyday ground coffee before making it. The delicate, spicy perfume and flavor of the cinnamon is a perfect ending to any meal. Or you can float a dollop of Cinnamon Whipped Cream on top of the hot coffee just before serving it.

Cinnamon Whipped Cream

Top hot coffee with a dollop of delicately flavored whipped cream. The cream slowly melts and flavors the coffee as you sip it. Use flavored whipped cream in place of plain whipped cream to enhance any dessert.

½	cup heavy cream
1	teaspoon cinnamon
1	teaspoon confectioner's sugar
½	teaspoon vanilla

With an electric mixer, beat the cream until it forms soft peaks when the beaters are lifted. Add the cinnamon, confectioner's sugar and vanilla and continue beating until the cream is stiff. Makes 1 cup.

Idea: To make Cinnamon Whipped Topping, thaw 1 cup frozen whipped topping, stir in 1 teaspoon cinnamon and ½ teaspoon vanilla.

Idea: Make Nutmeg Whipped Cream or Whipped Topping for eggnog or other drinks or desserts. Follow the directions for Cinnamon Whipped Cream or Whipped Topping, except omit the cinnamon and add ½ teaspoon nutmeg to the recipe.

Idea: Flavor whipped cream with your favorite liqueur—Kirsch, Amaretto, Grand Marnier, Frangelico, Kahlua, etc. For 1 cup whipped cream, beat in 2 to 3 teaspoons liqueur and 1 teaspoon confectioner's sugar. Serve over coffee or as a compatible dessert topping.

Clean Up

Some people are very neat and clean up as they cook. Most of us are not that wonderful, so be sure to allow plenty of time to tidy up the kitchen before your company comes. And don't forget to allow plenty of time to get yourself ready for your party.

Try to have the dishwasher emptied beforehand so you can put last-minute dishes and utensils out of sight. If you live in a small apartment or have a tiny kitchen with limited space, a large bin or laundry basket can come to the rescue. Load the dirty dishes, utensils, etc., in the basket and "hide" it in the laundry room, garage or an empty cupboard or closet.

This goes for dishes as you clear the table, too. It's fine to stack dirty dishes to make room, but the fastest way to end a party is to start cleaning up while your guests are still there. It's very ungracious and a considerate host or hostess doesn't do it. If there are lots of guests and dishes, you might consider hiring a teenager or someone to help with the clean up.

If we waited for the time to be right before we asked people into our homes, we'd never have anyone over. So make up your mind to just do it and learn from your experiences. And always remember, even if things don't turn out perfectly, everyone will still be very happy—because you cooked and they didn't have to!

 Everyday Hint: Clean and cook once and entertain twice! While you're in a party mood, invite different friends on two consecutive days and serve the same menu. Most shopping and preparation can be done for both parties at the same time. You'll get double use from flowers and everything is easier the second time around.

Menus

Special Occasion Dinner

This elegant do-ahead menu is just perfect for a special occasion or holiday sit-down dinner.

Toasted Pecans (p. 46)   Kir Royale (p. 148)

Bibb, Raspberry, Avocado Salad (p. 82)/Raspberry Vinaigrette (p. 82)

Chicken Cordon Bleu in Puff Pastry (p. 50)

Hollandaise Sauce (p. 66)

Frosted Grapes (p. 153)

Vegetable Terrine (p. 99)

Chocolate Mousse (p. 124)

Suggested Beverage:
White Wine such as Piesporter Michelsberg

Food Preparation Schedule

Up to a week ahead:
Make Chocolate Mousse and freeze.

Up to a day ahead:
Make Toasted Pecans and refrigerate.
Chill Champagne for Kir Royale; chill wine.
Wash and dry lettuce and refrigerate.
Clean and slice mushrooms for salad and refrigerate.
Make Vinaigrette and refrigerate.
Assemble Chicken Cordon Bleu in Puff Pastry and refrigerate
   (do not bake).
Make Frosted Grapes (or make a week ahead and freeze them).
Make Vegetable Terrine, cool and refrigerate.

Up to the morning of:
Prepare fresh berries for Kir Royale and refrigerate.
Slice avocados, dip in lemon juice and refrigerate.
Transfer Chocolate Mousse from freezer to refrigerator.

Before guests arrive:
Assemble salads on plates and refrigerate (add Vinaigrette just
   before serving).
Make Hollandaise and place in a Thermos.
Slice Vegetable Terrine, place on baking sheet and loosely cover
   with buttered wax paper or aluminum foil.
Whip cream for Chocolate Mousse and refrigerate.
Reheat Toasted Pecans and place in serving dishes.

Casual Get-Together

This easy menu is a real pleaser for TV watching, after backyard sports or when the gang drops by.

Savory Cheddar Cheese Spread (p. 30)
Apple Rings (p. 31) Crackers
Fried Pasta (p. 45)
Reuben Caraway Kraut Sandwiches (p. 44)
Dill Pickles
Marinated Vegetables (p. 84)
Minty Brownies (p. 130)

Suggested Beverage:
Soft Drinks or Beer

Food Preparation Schedule

Up to a day ahead:
Make Savory Cheddar Cheese Spread and refrigerate.
Cook pasta for Fried Pasta, drain well, toss with a few tablespoons
of oil and refrigerate.
Make Caraway Kraut and refrigerate.
Prepare vegetables and refrigerate.
Make Vinaigrette and refrigerate.

Up to the morning of:
Prepare Apple Rings, dip in lemon juice and refrigerate.
Mix together Vinaigrette and vegetables and refrigerate.
Assemble Reuben Caraway Kraut Sandwiches and refrigerate.
Make Minty Brownies.

Before guests arrive:
Fry pasta, drain and season. Place in serving bowls.
Cut Minty Brownies into squares.
Arrange Savory Cheddar Cheese Spread, Apple Rings and crackers on
serving platter.

Quick Dinner For Company

This easy-to-assemble menu works well for impromptu dinner guests, but it's even easier when you have a day's notice.

Red Radish Spread (p. 33) with French Bread
Caesar Salad with Caesar Dressing (p. 85)
Medallions of Turkey with Mushroom Tarragon Sauce (p. 58)
Rice
Buttered Carrots
Toasted Pecan Ice Cream Balls (p. 127)
Hot Fudge Sauce (p. 137)

Suggested Beverage:
White Wine such as White Zinfandel

Food Preparation Schedule

Up to a day ahead:
Make Red Radish Spread and refrigerate.
Prepare salad greens for Caesar Salad and refrigerate.
Make Caesar Salad Dressing and refrigerate.
Make Homemade Seasoned Croutons.
Clean and cut carrots for cooking and refrigerate.
Toast pecans, make Toasted Pecan Ice Cream Balls and freeze.
Make Hot Fudge Sauce and refrigerate.

Up to the morning of:
Make Medallions of Turkey with Mushroom Tarragon Sauce, cover,
remove from heat and refrigerate. (Reheat before serving.)

Before guests arrive:
Slice French bread and arrange on a platter with Red Radish Spread.
Assemble Caesar Salad ingredients in salad bowl (without dressing).

Buffet Dinner

When there are more people than table spaces, guests can help themselves to this sumptuous, easy-on-the-cook buffet.

Vegetable Tree (p. 150)
Hot Spinach Cheese Dip (p. 36)
Beef Stroganoff (p. 63)
Buttered Noodles
Vegetable Timbales (p. 98)
Sinfully Rich Chocolate Torte (p. 132)
Chocolate Leaves (p. 125)

Suggested Beverage:
Red Wine such as Burgundy

Food Preparation Schedule

Up to a week ahead:
Make Chocolate Torte and freeze.
Make Chocolate Leaves and freeze.

Up to a day ahead:
Prepare vegetables and endive for Vegetable Tree and refrigerate.
Prepare ingredients for Hot Spinach Cheese Dip.
Prepare Vegetable Timbales for baking and refrigerate.

Up to the morning of:
Assemble Vegetable Tree, cover with plastic wrap and refrigerate.
Make Beef Stroganoff (except do not add sour cream) and refrigerate.
   (Reheat before serving and add sour cream.)
Cook noodles, toss with butter and set aside. (Reheat before serving.)
Transfer Chocolate Torte from freezer to the refrigerator, decorate
   with Chocolate Leaves.

Before guests arrive:
Make the Hot Spinach Cheese Dip.
Arrange Vegetable Tree and Crudités on a serving platter.
Bake Vegetable Timbales.

Cocktail Party

Cocktail parties can be lots of fun—both to go to and to give. This flexible menu of hot and cold foods can be expanded or scaled down to accommodate the size of the crowd.

Herb Cheese Spread (p. 30)

Mushroom Almond Pâté (p. 32)

Assorted Crackers

Crudités (p. 34) with Squash Birds Garnish (p. 35)

Herb Mayonnaise Dip (p. 36)

Miniature Cheese Biscuits (p. 111) with Ham and Mustard

Chicken Parmesan Drumettes (p. 42) with Paper Frills (p. 155)

Spinach Herb Stuffed Mushroom Caps (p. 40)

Toasted Pecans (p. 46)

Chocolate Strawberry Tree (p. 158)

Coconut Almond Macaroons (p. 138)

Suggested Beverages:
Wine and Cocktails

Food Preparation Schedule

Up to a week ahead:
> Make Herb Cheese for Herb Cheese Spread and for Spinach Herb Stuffed Mushroom Caps and freeze.
> Prepare Cheddar Cheese Biscuit Mix (dry ingredients) and refrigerate or freeze.
> Cut up chicken wings for Chicken Parmesan Drumettes and freeze.
> Make Parmesan Bread Crumbs and freeze.
> Make Coconut Almond Macaroons and freeze.
> Make Paper Frills out of aluminum foil for Drumettes.

Up to a day ahead:
> Defrost Herb Cheese.
> Make Mushroom Almond Pâté and refrigerate.
> Prepare Crudités and Squash Birds and refrigerate.
> Make Herb Mayonnaise Dip and refrigerate.   (over...)

Up to a day ahead:

Slice ham for Cheddar Cheese Biscuits and refrigerate.
Make Cheese Biscuit dough, cut out, place on baking sheet and
   refrigerate.
Defrost chicken drumettes.
Make Spinach Herb Filling and refrigerate.
Make Toasted Pecans and refrigerate.
Chill beverages.
Prepare garnishes for beverages and refrigerate.

Up to the morning of:

Bake Cheddar Cheese Biscuits.
Make Chicken Parmesan Drumettes, attach aluminum foil frills.
   (Reheat before serving.)
Prepare Stuffed Mushroom Caps, place in baking dish and refrigerate.
Make Chocolate Strawberry Tree and store at room temperature.
Defrost Coconut Almond Macaroons.

Before guests arrive:

Arrange on serving platters and set out:
   Herb Cheese Spread and crackers
   Mushroom Almond Pâté and crackers
   Crudités, Squash Birds and Herb Mayonnaise.
Assemble Miniature Cheese Biscuits and Ham sandwiches.
   (Warm just before serving.)
Bake Stuffed Mushroom Caps.
Reheat Toasted Pecans.
Set out ice and garnishes for beverages.

Index